ELEVATORS, NEWSPAPERS, & POLITICS

Life in Kansas City, Missouri: 1890-1930

Sarah Jane Gross

Elevators, Newspapers & Politics: Life in
Kansas City, Missouri: 1890-1930/Sarah Jane
Gross

Includes biographical references

Abbreviations and shorthand in original documents are
spelled out in transcriptions for clarity and readability,
unless otherwise noted by [sic].

Front Cover Photograph:
Detail of main entrance of Graphic Arts Building at Tenth & Wyandotte,
Kansas City, Missouri, featuring terra cotta work; view facing west.
Photograph by Jeff Nichols, North Kansas City, Missouri, 2005.

Cover Page Photograph: "Mount, Nona"; box 84; reel 8;
*Leonard D. and Marie H. Rehkop Collection of Algert T.
Peterson Glass Plate Negatives* (C3888); The State
Historical Society of Missouri Research Center-
Columbia.

ISBN: (hbk) 979-8-9897449-3-0

CONTENTS

PROLOGUE

May 16, 1916
Kansas City, Missouri

Warren Bernard Harris had a habit of reading aloud from the paper in the morning as he smoked his pipe at the breakfast table. At that moment, he was engaged in reading the weather report. He had the morning edition of the *Kansas City Star* delivered to his door, gratis, every day. He rubbed elbows with the paper's staff and its proprietor, Mr. Nelson.[1] As a newspaper man himself, he was on good terms with others in the business and made a point of extending courtesy to the various news outlets regardless of political leaning. It was far more advantageous to make friends in this competitive industry. Thus, though he boasted ownership of the *Democrat-Herald* (a paper which espoused, predictably, Democratic views) he demonstrated civility and comradeship towards those of the Republican bent.

Indeed, in 1913, he brought the entire *Star* office a box of the 1911 crop of selected white barley which topped the Kentucky tobacco market. He had remarked, on that occasion, "The smile of some people is like a ray of sunshine and the frown of others is like a thunder cloud. Far better to smile and give cheer than to frown and cause unpleasantness."[2] He smiled now as he recalled this and glanced down at his pipe. He had cemented his lifelong camaraderie with the staff of the *Star* on that day. And he knew that the *Star* would stand by him should he require anything, whether in matters of business or of a personal nature.

---

[1] William Rockhill Nelson founded the *Kansas City Star* in 1880, as well as its morning edition, the *Kansas City Times*. Nelson was a newspaper man with money, and used his papers to influence Kansas City, MO social movements, ideas, and politics. His editorials through the late 1880s and early 1900s promoted park development and community improvement. His papers were widely distributed and widely read. The *Star* was aligned with the Republican party and, in the mid-to-late 20th century, expressed increasingly partisan views. Nelson himself was formerly a Democrat, and later shifted to Republicanism. For early biographies of Nelson and the impact of the *Star*, see *William Rockhill Nelson: The Story of a Man, a Newspaper and a City*, published by the staff of the *Kansas City Star* in 1915 and Ruth Evaline Lieber, "The Kansas City star as a social force," (Bachelor of Arts Thesis, University of Illinois, 1918).

[2] *Kansas City Times*, November 28, 1913.

His friends and family members fondly called him "W.B." for short, while those in the newspaper business referred to him as "Uncle Bernie." It was only his dear wife who called him "Warren," though she also liked "Bernie" when she was in the mood to tease him. He heard her footsteps approaching the kitchen just then, and he called her name. At the same time, he read the weather forecast from the paper, verbatim: "Missouri—Generally fair Tuesday and probably Wednesday, with moderate temperature." He glanced up and muttered to himself, "I would have said that the country is much too cool and unsettled to admit a rise in temperature." He smiled, tempted to share his play on words with a staff editor at the *Star*.[3]

He lived and breathed the printed word, having achieved a fluency with language in boyhood. By the age of nineteen, he became proprietor of a local Corning, Kansas paper and soon achieved greater ambitions. Several newspaper acquisitions later, he found himself with sufficient experience in managing and editing to secure a position as proprietor of several prominent papers headquartered in Missouri. He established roots and a name for himself in Higginsville, Lafayette County, Missouri, and served as foreman of the *Jeffersonian* for seven years.[4] During that time, he oversaw printing, editing, and the hiring of staff to do the meticulous and necessary work of feeding and bindery. Feeding—that is, the task of feeding sheets to the cylinder of a printing press—and bindery—the trimming, folding, and fastening together of papers—required skill and knowledge of the printing process. W.B. prided himself on training his staff well and promoting those who demonstrated particular talent. Handsome and confident, with a quick wit and sense of humor, he had no trouble attracting others to him.

He was also a man of intellect and foresight, but failed to predict that one female among his staff would prove herself his equal, if not his rival. Young and pretty, with a sharp wit and bright mind, Anna Floretta Mount began work at the *Jeffersonian* as a binder.

---

[3] "The Weather," *Kansas City Times*, May 16, 1916, page 1. The May 16, 1916 afternoon issue (*The Kansas City Star*, page 1) did indeed include the following weather report: "There is not much chance for warmer weather the next day or two, P. Connor, forecaster, says. It will be fair, but the rest of the country is too cool and unsettled to admit much rise in temperature."

[4] Walter Williams, ed., *A History of Northwest Missouri: Volume 2*, (The Lewis Publishing Company, 1915), 2019-2020. The *Higginsville Jeffersonian* was a weekly newspaper in print from 1890s through 1945. Prior to 1907, it was titled the *Jeffersonian*. See Library of Congress record for this paper.

Her dexterity with diction and her ability to arrange words to great effect won the attention of W.B. She was soon promoted to compositor and assisted in the paper's craftmanship.[5]

Though W.B. was loath to recognize it at first, this woman had won his mind and his heart in a way he never thought possible. Indeed, he had forsaken the possibility of marriage after his first wife had been taken from him. It had been cruel and debilitating to witness the typhoid snuff out her bright light. The first Mrs. W.B. Harris had partnered with him on the *Kelly Reporter*, which they founded in Vermillion, Kansas. After her passing in 1905, he devoted himself to his work. Others around him, including his colleagues at the *Higginsville Advance* and the *Kansas City Star*, admired his ambition and yet detected a persistent sadness behind his eyes.[6]

After his first year steering the *Jeffersonian*, however, his eyes began to change. In 1907, a playful light shone in them as he went about town, and his editorials were full of quips. And soon, it became apparent that someone had taken up his attentions; that someone was responsible for the enhanced quality of the paper and for his brightened mood.

W.B. was smitten with Anna Mount, and she with him. They lived in a world of their own: a world full of words, light, wit, and charm. Both were such skilled wordsmiths that their conversations never ran dull. They acted on whim and intuition, and in this spirit, they found themselves at the home of Reverend R. L. Pyle on the evening of December 12, 1908.[7]

The reverend officiated their marriage on that happy, wintry night. They had not notified friends or family of their plans, and thus had the night blissfully to themselves before making the announcement the following day.

---

[5] *The Lexington Intelligencer*, December 25, 1908, page 2; *Johnson County Star*, December 25, 1908, page 2.

[6] Williams, *A History of Northwest Missouri: Volume 2*, 2019-20; *The Reporter (The Kelly Reporter)*, December 24, 1903, page 4; "Mrs. W.B. Harris Dead," *The Corning Gazette*, June 22, 1905, page 8. W.B. Harris married Gertrude Warner in 1898 in Kansas. Gertude passed from typhoid in 1905, and W.B. then moved to Higginsville, MO.

[7] *The Lexington Intelligencer*, December 25, 1908, page 2.

Anna's parents, Charles and Samantha Mount of Higginsville, were pleased with the match, having known of the Harris farming family of Corning, Kansas, and having witnessed W.B.'s success in newspapers.[8]

Everyone was thrilled for the couple, apart from the disgruntled editor of the *Jeffersonian* who bemoaned the loss of his best employee. The Christmas day issue of the *Johnson County Star* reported,

> "Miss Mount had been an employee of the Jeffersonian for seven years and although Editor Coe is bewailing his loss he is sure that if she is as good housekeeper as printer there will be no trouble from that source."[9]

W.B. and Anna found humor in this and spent that Christmas in the cheerful company of Anna's parents and her baby sister, Nona.

Portrait of W.B. Harris and Anna Mount-Harris, circa 1910. Author's collection of Mount-Harris photographs.

---

[8] Williams, *A History of Northwest Missouri: Volume 2*, 2019-20; *The Lexington Intelligencer*, December 25, 1908, page 2.

[9] *Johnson County Star*, December 25, 1908, page 2. Julius ("Jule") G. Coe was a well-respected and prominent newspaper man in Missouri. He was the editor of the *Jeffersonian* (Higginsville) from est. 1902 until 1909 and worked alongside foreman W.B. Harris. Prior to this, he managed papers in Warrensburg and Odessa. In the spring of 1909, he fell ill and passed away in May of that year. His obituary was published in the numerous MO papers. *See, e.g., The Marshall Republican*, May 28, 1909, page 6; *The Lexington Intelligencer*, May, 29, 1909, page 3; *Chilhowee News*, June 4, 1909, page 2.

Anna was closer to her youngest sister than anyone in the world. Nona Lenora Mount—known as "Nonie"—was the baby of the family in the most endearing sense of the word. At the age of eighteen, she still resided with her parents and enjoyed a rather sheltered life in their home. The family had just moved to 1509 Harrison Avenue in the business district of Kansas City.[10]

It was quite common for residents of Higginsville to move to Kansas City for employment, and Mr. Charles Mount had done so to secure employment as an engineer. Such opportunities were especially ripe in the bustling downtown area.[11]

W.B., increasingly devoted to Anna and her happiness, took Nonie under his wing and offered her a printing job at the *Jeffersonian*. Anna was thrilled, and both she and W.B. extolled the virtues of the publishing industry and what a fine career she could make of it—just like W.B and Anna had done. Nona looked up to Anna and genuinely liked W.B., so she agreed with the plan and began what she supposed would be a long career in printing.

Eight years and a great deal of life experience later, Nona was indeed still in printing and worked for the Campbell-Gates Printing Company.[12] W.B. served as the proprietor of the Clay County-based *Democrat-Herald* and as the

---

[10] See 1910 United States Federal Census for Nona Lenora Mount. Year: 1910; Census Place: Kansas City Ward 8, Jackson, Missouri; Roll: T624_786; Page: 1b; Enumeration District: 0098; FHL microfilm: 1374799; See also U.S. City Directory listing for Nona Mount (Kansas City, Missouri, City Directory, 1910). Street Address: 1509 Harrison; Residence Place: Kansas City, Missouri; Occupation: Binder.

[11] Vi Bielefeldt and Janice McMillian, *Historic and Architectural Survey of Higginsville, Missouri* (Show-Me Regional Planning Commission & Missouri Office of Historic Preservation, 1982), 2; James R. Shortridge, "Maturity in a Railroad Mode, 1893-1933" in *Kansas City and How It Grew, 1822–2011* (University Press of Kansas, 2012), 61-62. See U.S. City Director listing for Charles S. Mount (Kansas City, Missouri, City Directory, 1910). Street Address: 1509 Harrison; Residence Place: Kansas City, Missouri; Occupation: Engineer.

[12] Nona Mount is listed in the 1915 city director for Kansas City, MO as a feeder (i.e., a cylinder feeder). Her address at the time was 1202 Tracy Ave. Harrison, Troost, Virginia, and Tracy were adjacent residential streets in the business district of Kansas City. The Mount family and descendants resided in this vicinity through the 1900s. See Rand, McNally, & Co., "A New 11x14 Map of the Main Portion of Kansas City," 1895.
The Campbell-Gates Printing Company (proprietors William N. Campbell and George W. Gates) operated from the Graphic Arts Building since the time the building opened for tenants in 1915. See U.S. City Directory for Campbell-Gates. Residence Year: 1915; Street Address: 606 Graphic Arts Bldg.; Residence Place: Kansas City, Missouri; Occupation: Press Room.

advertising manager for the Nelson-Hanne Printing Company.[13] Nona had worked on the *Democrat-Herald* for some time, but, at the age of 26, she had grown tired of being babied by her brother-in-law. As much as she appreciated his guidance and intervention, she felt ready for more independence. Thus, when a position became open at Campbell-Gates in the brand-new Graphic Arts Building, she was compelled to take it.

The last words she heard from her brother-in-law on the morning of May 16, 1916 were not even his own. He was reading the weather report aloud from the *Star*, of all things, and she was too occupied with running out the door to stop and say goodbye to him. Her sister, Anna, had already left to take the boys to the park. Two beautiful, innocent little boys who had no idea that they were the product of scandal.

Nona did not think of that, though, on her way to Tenth and Wyandotte streets in downtown Kansas City. The air was crisp and cool, just as the forecaster had predicted, and she wore a fashionable long coat and scarf to ward off the chill.

---

[13] Williams, *A History of Northwest Missouri: Volume 2*, 2019-20; *The Lathrop Optimist*, January 9, 1913, page 3. Warren B. Harris purchased the *Democrat-Herald*, a Smithville, Clay County, MO newspaper, in December 1912. The paper was in production from 1889-1982. It was known, alternatively, as the *Smithville Democrat-Herald* or *DH*. See https://chroniclingamerica.loc.gov/lccn/sn90061622/.
Harris was appointed secretary and advertising manager for the Nelson-Hanne Printing Company in the fall of 1915. Nelson-Hanne was a St. Joseph-based printing house. See advertisement for Nelson-Hanne in *The Catholic Tribune*, June 6, 1907, page 5 as "commercial and catalogue printers, bookbinders, and stationers." See mentions of Harris working for Nelson-Hanne in, e.g., *St. Joseph News Press Gazette*, September 29, 1915 and November 3, 1915.

Kansas City, downtown: a general view of downtown parts of city and business section, circa 1906-1909 (State Historical Society of Missouri: Ruth B. Bush Postcard Collection).

10th and Baltimore Streets., Kansas City, Mo, 1909 (Library of Congress)

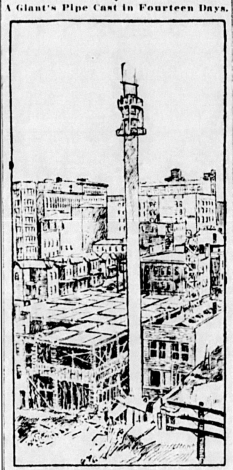

A Giant's Pipe Cast In Fourteen Days.

A detached smokestack that rises 135 feet has just been finished in the rear of the new Graphic Arts Building at Tenth and Wyandotte streets. The big stack is a continuous concrete tube 5 feet 8 inches in diameter. It was poured in fourteen days. Building these giant stacks is something of an art and certain contractors specialize in them.

The 8-story Graphic Arts Building will be finished July 1, S. B. Tarbet, the architect, said this morning.

Kansas City Star, May 19, 1915.

Her boots clicked satisfyingly on the pavement, and she felt proud as she approached the imposing and elegant edifice where she worked.

The Graphic Arts Building had been constructed in 1915 and rose eight stories high.

To characterize the building as elaborate would be a disservice. Local architect Samuel B. Tarbet oversaw the construction, which began in the Spring. Although the building was originally designed as seven stories, a partial eighth floor was added with the acquisition of additional funding. The main entrance, through which Nona entered, was on Wyandotte, and featured an annex on the northwest façade.

The Graphic Arts Building would, in years' time, be added to the National Register of Historic Places. The description of the edifice by the United States Department of the Interior narrates the artistic architecture in detail:

The deeply recessed, centrally placed entrance features a double-leaf wooden door with wide terracotta surround and is flanked by a prominent, fixed window at the north and a single-leaf wood and glass door at the south. The entry bay features geometric patterned, deeply recessed terracotta paneling, and stylized keystone above the entrance. Flanking the entry bay is basket weave patterned terracotta placed around geometric styled brackets while the whole is crowned by a wide entablature with the words "GRAPHIC ARTS BUILDING" carved into the frieze. A slender stringcourse separates the first floor from the shaft of the building.[14]

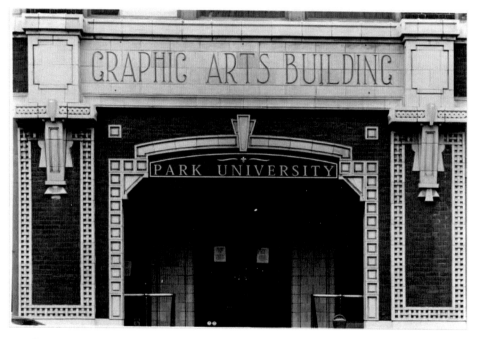

Detail of main entrance terra cotta work; view facing west. Photograph by Jeff Nichols, North Kansas City, Missouri, 2005.

In 1916, the Graphic Arts Building was indeed brand-new and magnificent, and served as headquarters for the Kansas City Graphic Arts Organization. It became an anchor for the graphic arts industry and the center for commercial

---

[14] United States Department of the Interior: National Park Service, *National Register of Historic Places: Graphic Arts Building, Jackson County, Missouri* (Architectural and Historical Research, LLC: Kansas City, MO, 2005), 2.

printing and its associated trades in Kansas City. The building's tenants included suppliers of paper and ink, printers and engravers, and even photographers and filmmakers. The core purpose of the building was to promote the printing industry, and thus the main floors were occupied by printing companies, stationers, lithographers, engravers, typesetters, photographers, and print supply houses.[15] Campbell-Gates Publishing Company, the prominent printing house where Nona was employed, operated from the sixth floor.[16]

Tarbet, the architect, prepared the design plans with the knowledge that the building would need to accommodate large printing presses. The floor was constructed to tolerate a load of 250 pounds per square foot, with a thirty-five percent impact. To account for the risk of paper flammability, Tarbet also incorporated a sprinkler system and an extra-large roof tank with a water holding capacity of 100 tons.[17]

Another necessary architectural consideration was elevators. The city contracted with Otis Elevator for an elevator system that consisted of a passenger elevator with a 2,500-pound capacity and two freight elevators with 5,000-pound capacity each. Steam heat was installed, as well as the most modern plumbing fixtures for the period. Each of the seven floors and the basement contained 9,500 square feet of floor space. The cost was estimated at $150,000.[18]

Nona used the passenger elevator daily to ascend to the sixth floor and descend to the first. Usually there was a skilled operator present to ensure the cage closed properly and that all mechanisms otherwise functioned. On that day, as she entered the Graphic Arts Building and glanced at the elevator, she felt a flicker of misgiving in her chest. She was not sure why and turned her attention to the fellow at the front desk who had waved to greet her. Out of the corner of

---

[15] Id. at 6-7.

[16] See U.S. City Directory for Campbell-Gates.

[17] *National Register of Historic Places: Graphic Arts Building, Jackson County, Missouri,* 7; see also newspaper coverage in *The Kansas City Star,* e.g., from March 7, 1915; May 19, 1915; and August 10, 1915.

[18] Id. Otis Elevator was arguably the largest national elevator company, established in 1853. It contracted with businesses around the world to install elevator systems. It published numerous booklets detailing its history, including, e.g., *Otis Elevator Company : the Otis elevator industry comprises large manufacturing plants in the principal cities in the United States, Canada, Great Britain, Germany and France* (1903); *Otis hand power elevators* (1920); and *The first one hundred years* (1953).

her eye, she caught the glint of gold as the sunlight reflected the bars of the elevator cage. She also caught a glance of a boy hovering in the shadows. He was small and could have been only nine or ten years old. He looked familiar, in an odd and disquieting sort of way. When she turned her head to get a better look at him, though, he vanished.

When the usual operator asked her if she was ready to go up to the sixth floor, she had half a mind to decline and tell him she felt ill. She shook away the silly thought, nodded to the operator, and proceeded upwards to the Gates offices. At the end of the day, she always looked forward to seeing Anna and hearing the news from W.B.; oddly, she began thinking about that while on her ascent in the elevator.

The main (east) and south facades; view facing northwest. Source: The Kansas City Post, December 31, 1915, page 13: "The new Graphic Arts Building, 930-40 Wyandotte Street, was one of the buildings finished this year and is now being occupied. It cost $97,000." Note, other reports estimate the cost at $150,000., see, e.g., The Kansas City Star, March 21, 1915.

Fig. 17. Horizontal Cylinder Hydraulic Elevator.

Otis Elevator Company, *Otis Elevator Company: the Otis elevator industry comprises large manufacturing plants in the principal cities in the United States, Canada, Great Britain, Germany and France* (1903), 32-33.
Figure 17 depicts the "Otis Hydraulic Elevator horizontal cylinder, designed for buildings where it is deemed advisable to install all of the elevator machinery in the basement... The illustration shows, in connection with the elevator, a compound-duplex elevator pump, compression and discharge tanks and the necessary piping connections. The tanks are here shown in the basement, but in large plants especially, it is often found more convenient to place the compression tank in the attic."
This type of elevator was most likely installed in the Graphic Arts Building based on the time period and the architectural description.

W.B. received a call at his office from Anna, late in the afternoon that day. She had taken the boys for an outing at the park, but she cut the visit short. Some of the other children were bullying them, she had explained, and so she had gathered them up and took them home. "Well, some young children are full of mischief. And a spoiled child may be very fresh," WB replied. Anna agreed and told W.B. that she had no desire for the boys to have any part in mischievous and cheeky behavior.[19]

She felt the need to speak to Nona, and placed a call to Campbell-Gates, sixth floor, Graphic Arts Building. She asked to speak with Nona. A man replied, in a tone that was gruffer than Anna expected, that Nona was busy and would soon be clocking out for the day. Before Anna could offer a curt retort, the line went dead. She felt, oddly, like she wanted to go down to Wyandotte and bring Nona home herself. But she had the boys with her and W.B. was not yet at the house. So, she sat down in the living room with them and cheered them up by telling jokes, and otherwise hiding the unsettled feeling in her chest.

Nona had worked a full day and was quite ready to collect her things and leave as the clock struck a quarter to five. To her great frustration, her employer, William N. Campbell, held her back. Nona listened with only half an ear and uttered a disinterested, "goodbye," when Campbell released her five minutes later.

It was 4:55p.m. by the time Nona reached the elevator. Her heart skipped as she looked at her watch. What time did the operators go home, and where was her usual operator? On most days, she entered the elevator at 4:45p.m. exactly, but now she was made late.

---

[19] W.B. often spoke in quips, or plays on words. Here, "fresh" means cheeky or impertinent. See *Kansas City Times*, Jan. 5, 1915, quoting: "Uncle Bernie Harris of Smithville is struck by the paradox that a spoiled child may be very fresh."

A moment later, a young man exited from the elevator and notified her that he could take her down to the first floor. "Are you a new operator?," Nona had asked as she cautiously entered the cage. She was uncertain even when he answered, "Yes," and proceeded to close the door.

The moment the elevator began to ascend to the seventh floor, Nona knew something was wrong. She also noticed that she was not alone in the elevator. There was a boy hovering in the shadows. It was the same boy she had seen just that morning. "Let me out please. Let me out now," she muttered, staring hard at the operator.

He seemed to detect the hardness and panic in her tone, and immediately stopped the elevator by placing the car on "safety" as it passed a foot above the seventh floor. He helped Nona out of the elevator and left the controller on "neutral." He asked her to wait while he went to the loft to release the car from "safety" so that they could go down.

In that moment, she was not sure whether it was the operator or the boy in the shadows that had told her to wait. All she knew was that she was tired and ready to go home, so much so that she was overcome by a sensation of falling forward. A desperate panic flooded her chest as she thought about Anna, W.B., and the boys, and her parents, all waiting to catch her as she fell.

CHAPTER 1

Autumn 1910
Higginsville, Missouri

Nona Lenora Mount was the youngest of the eight Mount children. Her parents, Charles and Samantha, had married young and moved from Moniteau County to Lafayette County, Missouri in 1880. William was the firstborn (1872) and was nearly twenty years Nona's senior. Next came Belle (1874), Stella (1877), and Elizabeth (1878), who were, to Nona, very grown-up and mature with full lives of their own.

Anna (1882), Mamie (1886), and Edna (1887) followed. Mamie left them in 1903 to marry a man who worked on cars. Thus, Nona, born in 1890, grew up with Anna and Edna. It was Anna, though, who loved baby Nonie from the first instant. It was Anna who crouched alongside Nonie as she learned to walk and promised to catch her if she fell. And Nonie fell in love with her big sister, growing as attached to her as a hummingbird to a flower.

It was easy to love Anna, and easy for Anna to love. Of all the Mount girls, she was the most maternal. She doted on Nona and Edna, and especially doted on their mother. Samantha Mount was a stoic woman and did not need tending to, but her heart softened whenever Anna was nearby. She allowed her to fuss and take care of things, and she was proud of the mature young woman Anna had become. Anna was quite the second mother to Edna and Nona, and it was her influence and kindheartedness which shaped them.

Matrimony did not change Anna's presence in their life one bit. If anything, her marriage to Warren B. Harris enhanced her bond to both Edna and Nona. Anna and Warren brought out the light and laughter in each other, and Warren was exuberant in welcoming the Mounts into his life. It was his idea, in fact, that the Mount women have their portraits done by a professional photographer in Higginsville.

"You ladies dress up and have your portraits taken by the best photographer this side of the Missouri river. He's a real talent. I'll drop you on my way to the office," he said one day when Nona and Edna were visiting the quaint home he and Anna shared in Higginsville.

"But what about…?" Anna began to protest—something to do with the work that needed to be done at the *Jeffersonian* that day—but Warren silenced her with a kiss.

"Don't worry about a thing, I've already taken care of it."

This caused Anna to laugh, her face lighting up, and she turned to look at her sisters. "Well, let's dress up, then, shall we? And, dear?" She turned back towards Warren. "Where are we going to have the portraits done?"

Warren smiled. "Peterson's studio, of course, on Russell Street."

With that, the plan was made, and Anna ushered Edna and Nona into the bedroom to help them choose gowns, hats, and jewelry.

Peterson's studio was in fact a photography studio located in central Higginsville. The proprietor, Algert T. Peterson, had established the studio in January 1909 after moving to Higginsville from Yazoo, Mississippi. As reported in Mr. William Young's history of Lafayette County, Missouri (1909-1910), in a short period of time, Peterson "had won for himself a reputation for the excellent quality of his work, both in the mechanical details and in the effects secured by careful attention to posing. He is an artist in his line and not merely a mechanical photographer."[1]

---

[1] William Young, *Youngs history of Lafayette County, Missouri* (Indianapolis, IN : B.F. Bowen & Co., 1910), 715-16.

Exterior of Peterson Studio on Russell St., Higginsville, MO., and the house next door. Glass plate negative taken by Peterson himself, circa 1910.

Indeed, by early 1910, Peterson had become well-established as the city photographer. Warren B. Harris made his acquaintance in 1909 and was impressed both by Peterson's craft and by his keen ability to relate to people. Harris casually spoke about him to J.G. Coe, the *Jeffersonian's* proprietor, and soon enough a paragraph appeared in the paper, introducing Higginsville, Missouri's new community photographer. Talk spread quickly among the newspaper men, and, to Peterson's great surprise, folks began flocking to his studio on Russell, asking questions and requesting to sit for portraits.

Peterson was a modest and reticent man who did not care for such public attention. He politely declined interviews in 1909 and focused on preparing his studio. In doing so, he built his strong reputation in photography through his skilled use of glass plates to produce portraits.

The glass plate negative technology, in use from 1850 through 1920, involved glass rather than paper to produce prints. This allowed for sharper, more stable and detailed negatives. There were two types of glass negatives: the collodion wet plate and the gelatin dry plate. During Peterson's career (1909-1927), the silver gelatin-coated dry plate negative was the predominant form of photograph in production. Invented in 1873, it was the first economically successful and durable photographic medium. Gelatin was mixed with light sensitive materials, such as bromide of ammonium or potassium and nitrate of silver. This formed an emulsion that was then machine-coated in one step onto large sheets of glass. The coated glass sheets, or plates, would be laid on a level table to allow the emulsion to cool and set. The plates were then set in racks and placed in a drying room or box. This resulted in "dry negatives" that were developed in a dark room.[2]

GLASS BOTTOM DRY PLATE DEVELOPING TRAYS.

The dry plate developing tray and the type of camera used, 1880s-1920s.

For an early book on the science and technology of photographic processes in the 1880s, see <u>Photography in the Studio and in the Field</u> by Edward M. Estabrooke (published Jan. 1887 by E. & H.T. Anthony & Company).

THE CAMERA FOR NEGATIVES, WET OR DRY.
CLIMAX IMPERIAL CAMERAS.

[2] Cornell University Division of Rare & Manuscript Collections, "Dawn's Early Light: The First 50 Years of American Photography; Exhibition: Photographic Processes: 1839 – 1889 DRY PLATE NEGATIVE (gelatin dry plate), 1880-1920, https://rmc.library.cornell.edu/DawnsEarlyLight/exhibition/processes/dry_plate_neg.html.

The Peterson Studio on Russell Street was designed in such a way as to fill the room with rays of light falling at an angle to illuminate the visage of the person sitting for a portrait. As noted in a leading book on photography—a book that Peterson may have studied—skylights, sidelights with north exposure, and the arrangement of shades could create the most charming effects of illumination.[3]

Interior of Peterson's studio on Russell St., Higginsville, MO. Glass plate negative taken by Peterson himself, circa 1910.

By 1910, Peterson could no longer rebuff the interview requests of reporters from the *Jeffersonian* and the *Star*. The *Jeffersonian's* Lee Shippey—an employee of Harris—ventured to Peterson's studio and procured enough material to pen an article in the paper's next issue. Peterson, still modest, agreed to the story being printed on the assurance that the paper would respect his personal privacy. Shippey reluctantly agreed, but referred to Peterson's reticence in the final edit:

---

[3] Edward M. Estabrooke, *Photography in the Studio and in the Field* (Jan. 1887: E. & H.T. Anthony & Company), 80-84.

> While nosing around Higginsville for news to fill the Jeffersonian, Lee Shippey found material for this story: "A. T. Peterson will not tell his name, but he believes the most hen-pecked man in Lafayette lives within a few miles of Higginsville. Mr. Peterson is getting famous for his baby pictures and almost every day babies are brought to him to be photographed, often from Lexington and other towns which have photographers of their own. The other day a couple from about seven miles out in the country drove in with their baby. As she was dressing the baby for the picture the mother called from the dressing room: 'Henry, I've brought the white stockings by mistake. Baby looks so much cuter in his pink ones. You'll have to drive right home and get them.' And without a word of protest Henry drove home, returning four hours later with the pink stockings.

Reprint of story in the *Kansas City Star*, June 10, 1910.

Reprints of the story soon appeared in the *Kansas City Star* and the *Lebanon-Rustic Republican*.[4] Peterson's status as a skilled photographer increased tenfold, and his sociability and business sense blossomed as a natural consequence. In the meantime, Warren B. Harris smiled and laughed at the spark he had created. He arranged for a portrait to be taken of himself and Anna and forged a friendship with A.T. Peterson during the sitting.

Peterson would take portraits of many Mount family members from 1910 through 1920.[5] It was his pleasure to do so, he would tell Warren, and he was more than willing to host Mrs. Anna F. Harris and the extended family whenever they desired. Thus, it took no effort at all for Warren to arrange the portrait day for the Mount sisters.

---

[4] *Kansas City Star*, June 10, 1910; *Lebanon Rustic Republican*, August 4, 1910.

[5] See Appendix for glass negatives of the Mount family and descendants, taken by Peterson between 1910 and 1920. These negatives are part of the Leonard D. and Marie H. Rehkop Collection of Algert T. Peterson Photographs, housed at the State Historical Society of Missouri-Columbia. See finding aid for the collection: https://files.shsmo.org/manuscripts/columbia/C388.pdf.

Anna, Edna, and Nona arrived at the studio mid-morning on that bright autumn day in 1910. Warren drove them the short distance to Russell in his Model-T on his way to his office at the *Jeffersonian*. Nona was dressed in a lace blouse with a broach fastened at the neck and a long dark skirt. She wore a knee-length cream-colored coat and gloves against the cold, at Anna's insistence.

"You can take the coat off when you're inside the studio, dear," Anna had said, and then smiled in satisfaction when she realized that Nona's attire matched hers almost exactly. Edna sat in between them in the car, absentmindedly fiddling with a ruby pendant necklace she had selected from Anna's jewelry box. As was her habit, she fell into a daydream, and looked up in surprise when the Model-T halted to a stop in front of the studio.

Warren helped the ladies from the car, and then looked at Anna in that special way of his before leaning to whisper in her ear. Whatever he said made her smile; Anna did not share it with her sisters, but her face was bright and beautiful for the entire morning. It was no wonder, Nona had thought, that Warren had fallen in love with her.

Peterson greeted them with a paternal warmth that was an instant comfort and shook hands with Warren, confirming that he would take individual portraits in as many variations of lighting and accessories as the ladies liked. Warren was satisfied and bid them goodbye, promising to return later in the afternoon. The sisters looked around the studio, taking in their surroundings. Though the space was small, it was well-furnished with a variety of lenses and camera boxes. A camera stand stood in the center of the room, and about the room were various accessories: flowers, tables, chairs, draperies, and boxes full of hats, gloves, and scarves (men's and women's).

"Here, I'll show you some examples," Peterson offered, slipping into the back room to fetch a box filled with glass negatives. There were numerous individual and family portraits carefully preserved in the box, including portraits of his own family. He adored his wife, and it was no doubt that she was his favorite subject by the number of negatives that featured her. Angnette Nelson-Peterson ("Nettie) was a striking young woman with petite features. She and

Algert had married in Illinois on August 6, 1908, having bonded over their shared Swedish ancestry.[6] Nettie was an expectant mother in 1910. Neither of them knew, on that fall day, that the child would be a precious little girl. Their daughter would be born in December of that year. They would christen her "Anna Louise" and she would become a prominent subject of her father's photographs. Algert would cherish and spoil her, and Nettie too, for the little girl would be the center of their world.[7]

Above: A.T. Peterson with daughter Anna Louise, circa 1913.
Right: Nettie Peterson with daughter Anna Louise, circa 1913.

Anna Mount Harris would also realize that she had room in her heart for a child after the Petersons welcomed baby Anna Louise. At that moment, however, her thoughts were solely on her sisters. She insisted that Edna and Nona sit for individual portraits first.

---

[6] Young, *Youngs history of Lafayette County, Missouri*, 716; 1910 U.S. Federal Census record for Algert and Nettie Peterson, Thirteenth Census of the United States, 1910 (NARA microfilm publication T624, 1,178 rolls). Records of the Bureau of the Census, Record Group 29. National Archives, Washington, D.C.; marriage record for Algert T. Peterson and Angnette Nelson. Ancestry.com. *Illinois, U.S., County Marriage Records, 1800-1940* [database on-line]. Lehi, UT, USA: Ancestry.com Operations, Inc., 2016.
[7] The 1920 U.S. Federal Census lists Algert, Nettie, and Anna Louise residing in Higginsville on Russell Street. Anna Louise is listed as daughter, age 9. The U.S. *Social Security Applications and Claims Index, 1936-2007*, lists Anna Louise Peterson with a birthdate of December 29, 1910.

Edna sat quietly for a classic portrait and declined to pose with scenery or to sit beside either of her sisters. Nona, on the other hand, was thrilled by Peterson's suggestion to capture her with background scenery, in addition to taking her portrait side-by-side with a portrait of Anna. Peterson selected feathered hats for them to wear, and provided Nona with a mink stole to wear for the scenic portrait. The session took several hours, and the sisters were all pleased with the result.

Portraits on prior page: Top left: Nona Mount; top right: Anna Mount; Bottom: mirrored scenic photographs of Nona Mount. All portraits are part of the Leonard D. and Marie H. Rehkop Collection of Algert T. Peterson Photographs-SHSMO-Columbia.

Anna was the most satisfied with how the portraits turned out. Later that evening, Warren winked as if to say, "I told you so," and suggested, "Why not have your mother sit for a portrait? It should be a family photo—the Mount women—with all of you around her, don't you think?"

Anna and Nona instantly agreed, but Edna was more hesitant. She was eager to return home to Kansas City, but not to collect their mother. She had social engagements that she simply could not miss. Anna had turned to glare at her and held her tongue only because Warren placed a hand on her arm and cast her a warning look.

Both he and Anna were keenly aware of the power of words to heal or harm, and Anna stayed quiet for fear of saying something she might later regret. Nona was still so young and ignorant of meaningful glances. She did not catch on to Edna's surliness on the trip back to Kansas City, or to the shared glances between Warren and Anna. Nona took Edna's words that she had "social engagements" at face value; Warren and Anna knew better.

When they all arrived at the Mount residence, Mr. Charles and Mrs. Samantha Mount were pleased to receive them. Mrs. Mount warmed at the idea of sitting for a portrait with her daughters and was soon drawn into lively conversation and embraces from Anna and Nona.

Edna disappeared to meet friends, but not before Warren delivered a perceptive glare of admonishment as he watched her leave. Ever since marrying Anna—in fact, as early as 1906 when he began to show interest in Anna—Warren had asserted protectiveness over the Mount women. He was, in many respects, the head of the family as much as Mr. Charles Mount. The elder Mount was aging and could no longer keep up with his children as well as he used to. As a farmer and a Civil War veteran, he was too proud to admit this. But, when Warren fit so naturally into the family and demonstrated such devotion to their wellbeing—well, it was only right that Warren step in and keep an eye on his girls.

Warren did have some influence, but the Mount women were of independent and stubborn stock. He knew that, once their minds were made up, there was nothing he could do to make them change course.

On that afternoon, Edna Mount met a man named Frank Stamm, a New Yorker just passing through Kansas City. Their flirtations would lead to marriage in the coming months.

On that afternoon, Nona Mount would make the formal acquaintance of a neighbor on Troost Avenue. He was young and handsome, with charismatic eyes and an easy charm that both thrilled and embarrassed Nona. His name was Charles Blake, and he had ambitions to be an actor.

On that afternoon, Anna Mount also made the acquaintance of the Sauvains, a Kansas City family. Guy P. Sauvain was a sharp and witty businessman. He worked alongside his father, John, in the shoe business. His mother, Laura, who had remarried to a man named "Schooling," was an independent businesswoman herself. At the time, Anna did know what line of business Laura was involved in. She would, in time, find out.

Glass negative of Mrs. Samantha Mount with daughters Nona Mount (left) and Anna Mount-Harris (right), 1910. The photograph shows evidence of fading over time.

Peterson's breadth of work from 1910 through 1920 was substantial, and his reputation as a well-known and highly respected photographer only grew. The War Department appointed him as the official photographer of Lafayette County during World War I. See The Concordian, November 14, 1918, reprinting a story from the Jeffersonian:

A. T. Peterson has been appointed official photographer for this county by the war department, the appointment being made on November 6 and reading "for the remainder of the war with Germany." On November 11 it was over. Mr. Peterson has some good pictures of war activities here. The office is an honor and he will receive recognition from the war department.—Jeffersonian.

CHAPTER 2

1911-1912
Kansas City, Missouri

By the late 1880s, the population of Kansas City, Missouri totaled 132,716 residents, making it the nation's twenty-fourth largest urban center. By 1900, the population nearly doubled to 163,750, making Kansas City the most rapidly developing city in the state. The system of parks and boulevards revitalized the city and contributed to economic growth, as did the development of railroad lines. The business district expanded, comprising the commercial hub of the city to the west including all manner of industries. The stockyard, packing, and wholesale industries generated significant income. As compared to other American cities conducting business in related industries, Kansas City was the leader in the Pullman railroad business; the sale of agricultural tools; yellow pine lumber; the hay market; farming territory; the tributary trade; park boulevards; winter wheat; and stock and feed cattle. By 1918, it boasted a large wholesale market. The arts industry (printing, publishing, and related fields) also burgeoned.[1]

The residential area of Kansas City, Missouri comprised of several adjacent streets. Pre-1900, Independence and Troost Avenues boasted fine, residential mansions. By the late 1910s, these streets lost their elite status to make way for modest and comfortable homes.[2]

William Rockhill Nelson, a Republican and editor of the *Kansas City Star* and *Times*, held a position of significant political influence and had a vested interest in the growth of the city. He used the *Star* as a vehicle to promote civic development as early as 1880. He advocated for the improvement of parks and boulevards, as well as innovations in public transport such as the jitney, in spite

---

[1] The Encyclopedia America (New York, Chicago: The Encyclopedia American corporation, 1904 and 1918 editions). See encyclopedia entries for "Kansas City".

[2] Shortridge, "Maturity in a Railroad Mode: 1893-1933" in *Kansas City and How It Grew: 1822-2011*.

of public opposition.[3] His friends and colleagues in the papers and in politics backed his proposals. In 1915, even W.B. Harris championed Nelson's cause and proposed a jitney line from Smithville to Kansas City.[4] Though not all of Nelson's efforts were met with resounding favor, he remained influential and amassed wealth through real estate development. His efforts were rivaled only by the entrance of James ("Jim") Pendergast and brother Tom in Kansas City in 1894.

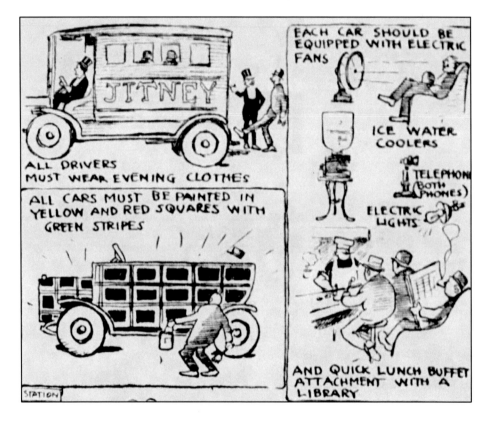

Cartoon in Kansas City Star, March 9, 1915, poking fun at the Kansas City ordinance which required jitney operators to furnished indemnity bonds and hyperbolizing its terms. Nelson and other jitney supporters correctly perceived the ordinance as a means of putting the jitney out of business.

---

[3] A jitney is a small bus used for public transport of groups of people. Nelson advocated for jitneys to support low-income workers in Kansas City who could not otherwise afford cars. This cause eventually failed in 1917 when Kansas City passed an ordinance requiring jitney operators to furnish indemnity bonds of $3000 for each car operated. Per the July 18, 1917 issue of the *St. Joseph News-Press*, (headline reads "Two Jitneys Left") this forced jitney operators out of business. See also myriad issues of the *Star* in 1915; and prior referenced biographies of Nelson.

[4] See *Kansas City Times*, February 16, 1915: "'Uncle Bernie' Harris of the Smithville Democrat-Herald is boosting for a jitney line from Smithville to Kansas City."

Geo. R. Lawrence Co., Kansas City, Missouri, business section. United States Kansas City Missouri, ca. 1907. Photograph. Library of Congress.

Jim Pendergast, a businessman from St. Joseph, became prominent in Democratic politics and asserted control over the business district through ownership of bars, saloons, and construction entities. Tom Pendergast won the seat as city alderman in 1911 following Jim's death and sought to control Democratic politics.

Tom ascended in Kansas City politics swiftly, following in his older brother's footsteps and building on the groundwork that Jim had so effectively laid. Jim had supported Kansas City's working class and the recreational activities they engaged in. He brokered deals in the "working class ward," whereby he protected vice industries such as gambling, drugs, and prostitution in return for a financial benefit. Tom embraced this business model and used his political clout to hire and fire workers. Though it was never openly acknowledged, everyone was aware that workers under Pendergast's jurisdiction put a portion of their salary into his pocket.

This was the making of the "Pendergast machine." Nelson and the Pendergasts were opposed on issues, and Nelson increasingly vilified Tom Pendergast in the *Star.*[5]

Portrait of Tom Pendergast, c. 1902
(from An Illustrated Description of
Independence, MO, p. 1963, 1902)

Albumen print of W.R. Nelson, c. 1897
(photographer D.P. Thomson, KC, MO)

During this shift in politics, women's roles also changed. Prior to the turn of the twentieth century, women assumed domestic roles, tending to the family and domestic duties such as cooking and cleaning. By the late nineteenth century, however, economic pressures and expansion compelled some families to send their daughters into the paid labor force, primarily in mills and factories. These women contributed their wages to support their families. Social perception of women in the workforce continued to evolve. By 1910, women comprised twenty percent of the U.S. labor force and could attain employment in offices, department stores, and restaurants. By 1920, twenty-six percent of

---

[5] See, e.g. Lawrence H. Larsen and Nancy J. Hulston, "Apprenticeship" in *Pendergast!* (University of Missouri Press, 2016): 38-39; Kimberly Harper, Stephanie Kukuljan, and John W. McKerley, "Historic Missourians: Thomas J. Pendergast." State Historical Society of Missouri. https://historicmissourians.shsmo.org/thomas-pendergast/; and biographies of William R. Nelson, e.g. *William Rockhill Nelson: The Story of a Man, a Newspaper and a City* (1915).

working women were employed as clerks, saleswomen, or stenographers.[6] Printing and publishing was a gentleman's trade, as evidenced by the social status of newspaper proprietors such as William R. Nelson (*Star*) and W.B. Harris (*Jeffersonian*).

Still, women were increasingly employed in clerical positions in the twentieth century as binders, cylinder feeders, and compositors. Women who demonstrated particular skill, and who married into a printing family—such as Anna Mount-Harris—progressed far more rapidly in the printing industry.[7]

Charles and Samantha Mount resided at 1509 Harrison in the residential area of Kansas City during this time. Nona and Edna lived with them, though both were working women and thus away from the house and from the watchful eyes of their parents. Edna worked as a clerk for the Motor & Machinists Supply Company, while Nona worked as a printer for Standard Printing Company. Both enterprises were in the congested Kansas City business district.[8]

The Blake family—James H. and Ada E. Crow Blake, and children Charles (age 20), Harriet (age 13), and Theodore (age 9)—resided one street up from the Mounts, on Troost Avenue. The family had moved to Kansas City from Crawford County, Iowa in about 1900. The Iowa Blakes worked in hotel management and farming, and a fair number of them owned real and personal estates of good value.

---

[6] Mary E. Odem, "'White Slaves' and 'Vicious Men': The Age-of-Consent Campaign" in *Delinquent Daughters: Protecting and Policing Adolescent Female Sexuality in the United States, 1885-1920* (University of North Carolina Press: 2000): 20-23, citing U.S. Census Bureau, *Sixteenth Census of the United States, 1940: Comparative Occupation Statistics for the U.S., 1870-1940* (Washington, D.C.: Government Printing Office, 1943).

[7] Lyndsey Claro, "Women in the gentleman's career of publishing." Princeton University Press. March 6, 2020. https://press.princeton.edu/ideas/women-in-the-gentlemans-career-of-publishing; see also newspaper advertisements for printing jobs during the early twentieth century. The *Kansas City Star* and *Times*, for example published "bindery girls wanted" ads.

[8] Kansas City, Missouri City Directory, 1911, listings for Edna A. Mount and Nona L. Mount.

James H. Blake worked in the wholesale vegetable industry for the Walter Commission Company to support the family. Son Charles was employed as an actor at the local theatre.[9]

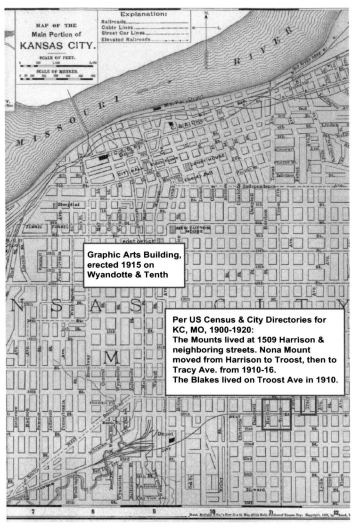

[9] 1900 U. S. Federal Census record listing: James H. Blake (age 29) born October 1870 in Iowa to Ohio and Pennsylvania-born parents is a shipping clerk who rents his home at 701 East 5th Street, 6th Ward, Kansas City, Jackson Co., MO. Living with him is his wife of twelve years, Ada Blake (age 32) born November 1867 in Iowa to Indiana and Illinois-born parents, with both of the children born to her still alive. Their children living at home were both born in Iowa to Iowa-born parents: Charles Blake (age 10) born April 1890; and Hattie Blake (age 2) born November 1897; See also 1880 Census records for the Iowa Blakes, and 1910 U.S. Federal Census record for Charles A. Blake, listing Blake family. US City Directory Listing for KC, MO lists James H. Blake working at 426 Walnut St. for Walter Commission Co. His residence was 1400 Troost Ave.

Charles Blake was born on April 20, 1890, and was just six days younger than Nona Mount, who was born on April 14th of that year. The two of them laughed over this when they met and struck up conversation in 1910. Living just a short block apart, Charles and Nona spent a good deal of time in one another's company. Their proximity made it easy to find opportunities to visit and converse, and they did so with increasing frequency over the subsequent months.

Charles was slender and handsome, and free-spirited. He was well-supported by his relatives, and his father did quite well in shipping and wholesale. Still, Charles wanted to strike out and make a career for himself in acting. His wit and easy-going nature charmed Nona. He grew tired sometimes and had to rest in the late afternoon. Nona thought nothing of this, and often joined him in reclining on the porch. They enjoyed each other's company, and Charles swiftly became infatuated with her. They were two people, both very young and innocent, who became caught up in each other with no real perception of the consequences.

It all happened very quick. On October 4, 1911, Charles applied for a marriage license with the State of Missouri, County of Jackson. The application was signed by Charles and his mother, Mrs. James H. Blake, before the county recorder. On October 5th, Jackson County issued a marriage license to Charles A. Blake and Nona Lenora Mount.

On October 5, 1911, Nona Mount delivered the news to her sister, Anna, and her brother-in-law, Warren, that she was married and with child.

Nona (Mount) Blake, circa 1911

The Mounts clustered around Nona during that time, but no one was as caring and devoted to her wellbeing than Anna. W.B. was right there alongside his wife, taking on the role of family protector (as was his way) and trying to brighten up Nona's days with quips that often found their way into the paper. Charles Blake hovered in the background, not sure what to do with himself or how to act around the Mounts. Nona's parents—Charles and Samantha— accepted him and strove to be on good terms with James and Ada Blake. There was no alternative, in their minds. What was done, was done, and the families must make the best of it. Mrs. Blake cared about both Charles and Nona, without a doubt. She impressed upon Charles the importance of doing the right thing. She and Samantha Mount came to a level of understanding that they would support their youngest children through this time.

W.B. Harris was a tad more skeptical and dubious of Charles and the Blakes' intentions. He tolerated Charles and practiced civility for Nona's and Anna's sake. He never said a critical or unkind word about him. At least, not within earshot of the ladies.

One afternoon, when Anna and Nona had retired to their rooms, he found Charles sitting on the porch, twirling his top hat in his hands. He had just returned from a rehearsal at the theatre. W.B. sized him up for a moment, his hands in his pockets, and then he stood across from Charles, leaning his back against the doorpost. Charles saw his shadow before looking up into his face. He straightened up with a jolt and murmured, "Mr. Harris."

W.B gave a slight nod and asked, "How are things in the acting business?" He meant it casually, as a way of making conversation. Charles seemed to take the question more seriously, however.

"All right some days, not others. I don't know how I'll manage to support Nona and the baby."

W.B. Harris breathed deeply, flaring out his chest. "You listen here, Charles Blake." His tone made Charles sit to attention again. "Nona will be cared for just fine by her family, and that includes me. Your job now is to be a good husband and father. I think you can do that because you've got no choice. But if you can't…" His voice grew quieter, and he stepped closer to Charles. The difference in their stature—W.B. fit and well-built, Charles small and thin—made it appear as though W.B. towered over him. "Then I'll run you out of town faster than you can blink."

The threat unnerved Charles for a moment, and he just nodded, sinking back into his chair, and waiting for W.B. to leave him be. Charles was more annoyed than anything. W.B. did not faze him. He was just a big newspaper man who liked to pretend he wielded more power than he possessed. So, Charles shook off the encounter and gradually forgot about W.B.'s comment. He did not realize then that W.B. was a man of his word who always made good on his promises.

❖

The months passed by, and Nona stayed confined to the house on Harrison under her parents' watch as the time to deliver the baby grew near. Meanwhile, Anna and W.B. carried on as usual, working at a lively pace to publish each issue of the *Jeffersonian*. W.B. also became involved in St. Joseph Advertising Clubs, cohorts of men in the print and publishing trades with expertise in news advertisements. In February 1912, he attended the annual convention of the Associated Advertising Clubs of America in Leavenworth, Kansas. He boarded a train with thirty other club members, taking the Missouri-Pacific line out of Union Station. Everyone wore a big red "St. Joseph Shows You" badge, and carried with them stacks of St. Joseph advertising material. W.B. enjoyed the experience, and when he returned home via a special Chicago Great Western car at two-o-clock in the morning, he was full of new knowledge and ambitious ideas.[10]

In his absence, Anna spent time with her new friends, the Sauvains of the Kansas City shoe business. There were three brothers and a sister, all close in age, and all with vibrant personalities. The sister, Eunice, was a budding actress and had dreams of going to New York to be on Broadway. The brothers—Paul G., Guy P., and J. Clyde---all worked in wholesale shoes alongside their father, John. It was a family business, and the men sure made a success of it. They were listed in all the papers and city directories.[11]

Their mother, Laura Prosser, had divorced John Sauvain and married Mr. Charles Schooling in 1905. He worked as a farm laborer and later as a barber. The boys remained close to Laura, nonetheless, and Clyde would reside with her and his stepfather during the 1920s. The boys always knew their mother to be an independent woman, and that never changed.

One afternoon, Anna and Warren hosted Guy and Paul Sauvain for lunch. They also invited Edna Mount-Stamm and her husband Frank Stamm. Edna had

---

[10] *St. Joseph News Press Gazette*, February 20, 1912, "Party to Leavenworth: St. Joseph Sends Creditable Delegation to Convention of Advertising Clubs."

[11] Eunice Sauvain-Skelly would move to New York in 1914, and starred in vaudeville-style shows. See, e.g., *The Buffalo Courier*, November 7, 1920 (Buffalo, NY), advertising a musical comedy show in which Eunice Sauvain starred. She married Hal Skelly in 1914 shortly after moving to New York—he was a well-known burlesque comedian, who starred in the shows alongside her. Census records and city directories list John, Paul, and Guy Sauvain in shoe sales.

married Frank in December 1911, and they continued to reside in Kansas City.[12] Anna considered Frank to be an amiable man, but he was not particularly handsome or engaging. Edna seemed comfortable with him, which is all that really mattered.

Paul Sauvain was rather serious. Guy Sauvain, the younger brother, was quite the opposite. He was witty, charming, and handsome, and he kept the conversation going for the entire afternoon. Everyone seemed to brighten around him, even Edna who was normally quite aloof. He spoke proudly about the family business and went on about the details of shoe repair for men's shoes (especially repair of the soles, about which he had special knowledge). He also boasted that he, Paul, and their father ran their shop with no interference from "aldermen Jim and Tom." Both Anna and Edna looked at Guy quizzically as he said this. Before Anna could question Guy's meaning, Warren intercepted with, "That's the St. Joseph spirit, you mean. That reminds me, gents, have you ever ridden on the Chicago Great Western? I had the pleasure just recently, coming home to Kansas City from Leavenworth…"[13]

The men were swiftly pulled into this conversation, leaving the sisters to sit there, bemused, until they excused themselves to fetch some more tea. Edna casually inquired about Nona, and Anna assured her that their youngest sister was safely at home with their parents. Edna had been mildly interested to hear of Nona's marriage, and surprised to hear about the coming baby. She had enough tact, however, not to speak of it, even in private with Anna.

"So, do you like him?" Anna said, interrupting Edna's train of thought.

"Warren? Of course I do, I always have. You two are a perfect match."

Anna frowned and batted Edna on the arm. "Not Warren, silly. Guy Sauvain. What do you think of him?"

---

[12] *Kansas City Journal*, December 22, 1911, listing marriage licenses: Edna Mount (Kansas City, MO, age 22) married to Frank J. Stamm (Brooklyn, NY, age 22).

[13] The Chicago Great Western Railway linked the Midwestern cities of Chicago, Minneapolis, and Kansas City, with each branch meeting at Oelwein, IA.

At this, Edna blushed slightly. She hated to admit it, but she did like him. She found him engaging and charming, and she liked the way his eyes twinkled when he laughed. And she felt exceedingly guilty about this. She was a married woman, for heaven's sake!

"I like him fine," she murmured evenly. "Frank does too, I think." She turned her head, listening to the men's murmur of conversation echoing from the other room.

Anna nodded, her lips lifting in an almost imperceptible smile. Guy Sauvain had made an impression on them all, it seemed. "Well, I wonder what he meant by that comment about his business not being…what was it? Interfered with by the aldermen."

Edna was just as clueless as Anna and shrugged, then glanced down at her wristwatch. "Oh dear, Frank will want to be leaving soon." As if he had heard her, Frank Stamm called her name and strode into the room. Edna glanced at Anna somewhat apologetically, and she and Frank began making their goodbyes. Anna watched the exchanges and noticed that Guy shook hands with Frank and gave Edna a winning smile.

"We shall have to do this again." Warren had appeared at Anna's side, resting a hand at her back. "Such lively company."

"Oh yes," Anna agreed softly, leaning against him briefly before joining Guy on the porch. Paul was already at the car.

Guy beamed, extending a hand and thanking her for her hospitality. "I must return the favor."

"Not at all," Anna replied. "Our pleasure, and we already look forward to another luncheon soon." She paused and lowered her voice. "You can tell me something, though."

"Oh, yes?" Guy's eyes flickered with interest.

"You said that the aldermen don't interfere with your business. Do you mean you don't have to pay dues to Pendergast?"

Guy's expression was unreadable, and at length, he broke out into a broad smile. "My, my, Mrs. Harris, you know more than you let on. That is what I mean. We are on the 'nice' side of the street. Now, my dear mother, on the other hand…"

"You never said what your mother's line of business was," Anna interrupted, feeling her heart hammer.

"No, I did not," Guy acknowledged slowly, and turned to look over his shoulder. His brother Paul was occupied in studying papers in the seat of their car and seemed to be in no hurry to leave. "Suffice it to say that she is beholden to Pendergast," he muttered quietly.

Anna held his gaze and demanded, "And what does she do?"

Perhaps it was the intensity in her expression, or the fact that Warren Harris was striding over. Guy was not sure what made him say it, but before he could stop himself, he heard himself say, "She helps fallen women."

Before Anna had time to respond, Guy waved to Warren, calling out that he and his brother were now late getting home, but that he would gladly call again.

Anna lay in bed that night unable to sleep. The wheels were turning. Guy—the alderman—fallen women—Nona and the baby. Unconsciously, her hand drifted to her middle and she gripped the material of her shift. A sad sort of sigh escaped her. Warren, who was asleep beside her, wakened, and moved to place his hand over hers.

"What is it, dear? Can't you sleep?"

When she stayed silent, he sat up, kneeling over her. In the dim light of the room, he could detect the glimmer of a tear on her cheek. He gently eased his thumb over her cheekbone, his expression softening. He knew what was bothering her even before she spoke.

"Nonie is going to have a child and I'm so pleased for her. And Nettie Peterson has her little girl. So why can't we? Why can't *I*?"

For the first time in their lives together, Warren had no answer for her. He could only hold her, whispering soothing words. They had tried to have a child to no avail, and in that moment neither of them knew the reason or the answer. Anna exuded maternalism—more so than any woman, in Warren's view—and the fact she was deprived of motherhood pained her and pained him in turn.

Sometimes answers are derived from unexpected places. Unbeknownst to Anna and Warren, the answer to the question---the answer to their prayers for a child—would have a great deal to do with Guy Sauvain and his mother.

CHAPTER 3

1912
Kansas City, Missouri

The baby was the light of Nona's life. When he arrived—a gorgeous little boy with eyes and nose and lips that were a carbon copy of hers—she was sure that he was a blessing after all. Within a few hours of holding him, she loved him more than anything and could scarcely remember life before him.

Her mother, Samantha, and her sister, Anna, were present for the birth. She had been scared and panicked despite their reassurances and did not calm down until the local physician arrived to tend to her. Dr. Frank Hurwitt was well-respected in Kansas City as a specialist in anaesthesiology. He had excelled while at Washington University in St. Louis and cared deeply about his patients. He had an office at 1500 Troost Avenue in 1912 and was well-known among residents in that vicinity. During his long and successful career, he would work with the city health department and welfare board; serve on the staff of the Research Medical Center, General Hospital, and St. Luke's Hospital; and enlist in the U.S. Army Ambulance Company during World War I. He would also serve as chief of anaesthesiology at the Menorah Medical Center, which would be established in 1926 by the Jewish community in Kansas City. Dr. Hurwitt was proud of his Russian-Jewish parentage.[1]

Nona never thought about a name for the baby during her entire pregnancy. Her mother had made suggestions, but she was disinterested and turned them down. But, when the doctor delivered the child safely, she knew then what she would call him. She had a name for her beautiful baby boy.

---

[1] US Census records for Frank Hurwitt, 1910 and 1920; US City Directory for Kansas City, MO, 1912, listing Frank Hurwitt as a physician at Troost and Prospect Avenues; obituary for Dr. Frank Hurwitt, *Kansas City Times*, February 1, 1975; U.S., World War I Jewish Servicemen Questionnaires, 1918-1921 for Frank Hurwitt (Series II: Questionnaires: Jews; Record Group Description: (G) Officers - Citations, Casualties (Box 16); Box #: 16; Folder #: 11; Box Info: Wounded: G-J).

"He is Frank Hurwitt Blake," she announced softly. She was tired, but so happy and relieved as she gazed down at the baby. Samantha and Anna did not question her.

"So, he is. Little Frank Hurwitt," Anna had agreed. She nestled down beside Nona, her heart bursting at the sight of this perfect boy. He had Nona's features, and looked exactly how Nona had when she was born. Anna remembered her sister's birth vividly and how she had felt a deep maternal instinct to care for her. She felt it again, looking down at the little boy. She also felt a deep longing—a longing for a child of her own. Anna had resigned herself, however, to the fact that she would not be able to bring a child into the world. She would just be the best aunt to little Hurwitt, she decided. And so she would be, in more ways than she could imagine.

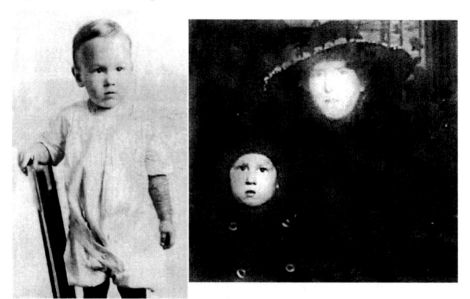

Left: Frank Hurwitt Blake, c. 1914. Right: faded photo of Nona Mount-Blake with baby Frank Hurwitt Blake, c. 1913. Photos courtesy of Michele Blake, daughter of Frank H. Blake.

Both the Mount and Blake family were thrilled to meet the baby. Charles Blake, as awkward and nervous as he was to become a father, surprised everyone by cooing and smiling over the boy and giving Nona more attention than ever. The three of them—Nona, Charles, and baby Hurwitt—made for a delightful and happy family in those early days. Samantha Mount and Ada Blake were always around, helping them adjust. Charles Mount, too, bonded with the baby immediately and boasted that he would teach him to swim and fish when he was a bit older.

Warren and Anna continued to make frequent visits as the months passed by. Anna was desperate to see Nonie and Hurwitt, and Warren likewise wished to see them. But he often had other reasons to visit Kansas City.

At that time, Warren had an interest in keeping an eye on Charles Blake. He was a man of his word, and needed to make sure that Charles was acting as a good husband and father should. When Nona and Charles stepped out for a walk, Warren would join them. Anna agreed to stay and watch the baby. Nona seemed to enjoy walking with Charles and Warren and would lock elbows with both of them, smiling joyfully as they strolled across the lawn.

Warren also took them out on drives in his Model-T—to the park, to the theatre, to the *Star* offices. Anna had encouraged these outings, telling Warren that he must make friends with Charles: "He is family now, after all. Do it for dear little Hurwitt's sake, if not for mine." Warren could not refuse her, for he could not stand to see Anna unhappy, let alone Nona and the baby. So, he kissed his wife and knelt to check the car engine while Nona and Charles strolled outside to join him. Anna captured a photograph of them on that day, using the camera that Algert and Nettie Peterson had given her as a gift.

Warren also had an interest in the Sauvains. Thus, on days when the young Blake family remained at the house with Anna, Charles Mount, and Samantha Mount, Warren made plans to meet with Guy Sauvain. After that first luncheon with Guy and Paul Sauvain, Warren had made inquiries with his contacts at the *Star*. They confirmed that the brothers were indeed in shoe sales. They also confirmed that their mother, Laura Prosser-Schooling, was associated with various Kansas City hotels, including the Armond Hotel at 406 E. 9th Street. Further discreet inquires confirmed that Mrs. Schooling had recently helped a young woman secure employment as a governess. This young woman had fallen on hard times and had a child she could not care for. She had no husband, and no other family, and the child was no more than two years old.[2]

---

[2] US City Directory for Lora Schooling, Kansas City, MO, 1911, working at or for "D'Armond Hotel, 406 E. 9th St." See "Help Wanted Ad" in the *Kansas City Star*, June 24, 1911, asking for a "governess—by young lady as governess" and listing the Armond Hotel at 406 E. 9th Street. The hotel business in Kansas City was controlled by the Pendergasts. Little is known about the reputation of the Armond Hotel, however other hotels in the vicinity (e.g., the Jefferson at W. 6th St.) were known as "assignation centers" for illicit activities such as gambling, alcohol, and prostitution. Larsen and Hulston, *Pendergast!* at 60-62.

Charles A. Blake, Nona L. Mount-Blake, and Warren B. Harris (kneeling beside car), c. 1912. Photo courtesy of Michele Blake.

Warren's meetings with Guy were tactful and discreet, often held at the Sauvain shoe store under the guise of contemplating a purchase of new boots. Through veiled language and creative metaphors, Guy confirmed that the rumors about the woman with a child were true, and that his mother was determined to place the child into a good home. Over the course of a few weeks, Warren met with Guy—three times at the shoe store, after which Warren was forced to buy a pair of boots, and three more times at the nearby park accompanied by a colleague at the *Star* who swore to secrecy.

On the last of these visits, an older and very attractive woman met them. Guy nodded, confirming her identity as his mother, Laura. In veiled and whispered terms, she said that the girl was working now as a respectable woman, and that she wanted nothing more to do with her past. In response to Warren's questions, Laura remained tight-lipped but assured him that the woman was just not able to be a mother and could not care for the baby. "It is a pleasing little child, and a real shame that it has no mother. It is under my care now, but it needs a mother, a father, a family." Her eyes flickered between Guy and Warren. "My son tells me that you and your wife are the right family."

Warren did not recall the exact details of what transpired later that afternoon. He only knew that he was driving back to the Mount home that evening, and that Guy P. Sauvain, Laura Schooling, and a baby boy were in a car right behind him.

Laura had said that it was a "pleasing little child." To Warren, that description was an utter disservice. The boy was as perfect and gorgeous as an angel, with vivid blue eyes and golden hair and skin like porcelain. He had been guarded and skeptical for weeks, but when Laura brought the child to him, the earth seemed to shift beneath him, and his breath caught in his chest. He had no words, no thoughts, only love towards this sweet and beautiful boy. There was no option but to take the child home. He had no idea what Anna would think, or how she would react, but he would take the child home. He simply had to.

When he pulled the car up to the house, Anna was already on the front porch saying her goodbyes to Nona, Charles, and little Hurwitt. Warren waited for Guy to pull up alongside him. He stepped out of his own car and found that his legs were shaking almost uncontrollably. He leaned against the door for support. His behavior, and likely the expression on his face, must have caused Anna concern, for she frowned and quickened her pace to reach him.

"Bernie, dear," Anna murmured, using a term of endearment. "Is something the matter? What is…?"

Laura chose that moment to step out of Guy's car. Guy stepped out right after her. Anna gasped in shock, looking from Guy to Warren. Before she could utter another word, Laura came close to her. It was only then that Anna noticed a bundle in her arms.

Anna's face turned white when she saw the golden head of hair and serene face of the child amidst the blanket he was wrapped in.

"Mrs. Harris," Guy's voice broke through her shock. "This is my mother. And this…" He gestured towards the boy. "This is your son."

Anna's voice was so hoarse she could scarcely make a sound. Instead, she turned to her husband, desperate longing and confusion in her eyes. Warren only nodded, stepping towards her with his legs still shaking until he could lean against her and whisper, "Our son, meet our son."

Neither of them was sure how it happened, but suddenly the boy was in their arms and Anna had tears streaming down her face as she kissed the child and leaned against Warren to keep from falling. At some point, Guy and his mother disappeared, driving away and leaving the Harrises to enjoy time as a family.

Warren and Anna would have both Guy and his mother over for lunch, and Anna would learn the full story of what had transpired and how she had been blessed with the perfect child. But, that evening, they were consumed with an unfathomable love for the boy who truly seemed to be the angelic blessing they had been waiting for.

❖

The Harrises stayed with the Mounts for several days. During that time, Charles Mount accompanied Warren to the county clerk's office to collect paperwork. No explanation was needed, and no questions were asked. Perhaps Guy or employees of W.R. Nelson had done it. But, when Warren arrived at the office, he was simply handed over papers confirming that he and Anna were parents to a boy born in Kansas City, Missouri, 1912.

They christened the boy Howard Bernard Harris. Howard was showered with love and attention from everyone in the Mount household. Nona had been thrilled with his arrival and sat him beside Hurwitt in the bassinette. She cooed over them both and exclaimed with joy that the boys would be like brothers and would grow up together. No one said a word or suspected anything. They all simply loved the boy and treated him as Anna's baby from the moment he crossed the threshold.

That was the Mount way, as Charles Mount explained. His own mother, Jane, had loved fiercely and welcomed any child into her home. "And so shall we, and so shall all the Mounts," he told Warren and Anna.

Left: Howard B. Harris, c. 1915. Right: Howard B. Harris, c. 1926

Harris family, c. 1920

CHAPTER 4

The fall and winter of 1912 were seasons of change for the Mount and Blake families. Nona and Charles Blake had grown restless. Though they adored baby Hurwitt and enjoyed parenting him, they both desired time away from the house. For Nona, that meant seeking out employment at another printing company. Samantha Mount had urged against it, telling Nona that her role was to be a mother now and that she had no need to work. As stubborn and determined as Nona still was, she would hear none of it and turned to her brother-in-law for support.

W.B. Harris was struck by the difference between his wife and Nona. He and Anna wanted nothing more than to spend every moment with their new son. Anna had craved motherhood for so long and wished to spend as much time as possible with Howard. If that meant resigning from her duties at the paper, then so be it, she had told Warren. Nona, on the other hand, was eager to return to work and to share childrearing duties with her parents. Charles and Samantha Mount doted on Hurwitt and were more than willing to help parent him. Meanwhile, Charles Blake was equally as restless as Nona. He was already back at the theatre, and otherwise at his parents' home and deep in discussion with his father, James Blake.

In any event, W. B. Harris was caught between the disparate preferences of his family members all while managing his own business affairs. The *Jeffersonian* had been a worthwhile and satisfying endeavor for the past seven years. His work there had shaped him as an editor and a businessman. He fostered fruitful relationships with others in the printing industry, on both a professional and personal level. His position had also led him to Anna, who was the best partner he could have ever hoped for. Yes, the *Jeffersonian* had been good to them both, but he sensed that his ambitions could take him further.

Of late, he had been spending time in St. Joseph for meetings of the advertising club and was moderately involved in the Kansas City Commercial Club. The aim of the Commercial Club was to support businesses that boosted the economy. It was not driven by politics; its members included those from both parties.[1] Through these activities, Harris learned that a local Clay County newspaper was afloat and in need of good management. His friends in St. Joseph urged him to consider the opportunity.

He did, and he could not turn it down. The *Smithville Democrat-Herald* was based in Clay County, about 20 miles from Kansas City. It had changed hands multiple times since 1909 and was in dire need of a new proprietor. After speaking with the staff and getting a feel for the paper, Harris knew that he was the man for the job. Especially once he found out that his colleagues at the *Jeffersonian* and the *Star* had sung his praises and recommended him. He would manage the paper alongside Edwin Forrest Livesay, a newspaper man local to Smithville. Livesay had purchased the paper in October 1912 alongside editor C.A. Lederer. Harris liked and respected Livesay from the start, and the two struck up an immediate friendship. They had many mutual friends in the business, including Lee Shippey of the *Jeffersonian*. This history, and the fact that they shared similar values, motivated Livesay to offer Harris the role of co-proprietor.

Messrs. E. F. Livesay and C. A. Lederer announced in last week's issue of the Smithville Democrat Herald that they had purchased that paper from J. H. Clark and also made their principal announcement. The Herald is one of the newsy newspapers of northwest Missouri and we predict a pleasant future for the new proprietors. Mr. Lederer will edit the paper.

The Lathrop Optimist, Oct. 24, 1912. Prior to Livesay's acquisition of the paper, the *Smithville Democrat-Herald* was owned by A.J. Summers (1909-1911); Thomas D. Bowman (March 1911-Dec. 1911); J.H. Clark (Dec. 1911-Oct. 1912); and Brooks Bradley (Feb. 1912-Aug. 1912). All were long-time newspaper men in Missouri.

---

[1] Larsen and Hulston, *Pendergast!* at 26-27, on the activities of the KC Commercial Club, citing, Frederick Spletsoser and Lawrence Larsen, *Kansas City: 100 Years of Business* (Kansas City: Kansas City Journal, 1988).

W.B. spoke over the matter with Anna, and to his relief, she supported him. She had no great desire to remain as compositor for the *Jeffersonian*. Like W.B., she too had given the paper seven good years, and she was agreeable to moving on. Her focus was on Howard, and on ensuring that she and Warren were in the best place—personally and professionally—to do right by him. To that end, Warren assured Anna that acquiring the *Smithville Democrat-Herald* ("DH") was professionally (and politically) advantageous to them. He further investigated the residential neighborhood and school in Smithville and judged them fitting for young Howard.

Thus, it was set. In December 1912, W.B. acquired the *DH* and would commence his duties in January 1913 after the holidays.

As usual, this news spread like wildfire throughout Kansas City and adjacent towns. The January 9, 1913 issue of the *Lathrop Optimist* (Clinton County, Missouri) printed the story on the right.

W. B. Harris, formerly of Higginsville, has purchased the Smithville Democrat-Herald and will hereafter be at the helm of that good ship. The Democrat-Herald has one of the best fields in northwest Missouri and Editor Harris will undoubtedly give the people of that community a paper to be proud of. Our best wishes to the D-H.

Friendly rivalry continued between W.B. and the editors at the *Kansas City Times* and *Star*, even more so once W.B. took on the mantle of proprietor of the *DH*. It was all in good fun, and W.B. thrived on the collegial sparring. The *St. Joseph-Gazette* (a constant ally to W.B.) reported the story on the right in its January 14, 1913 issue.

Steve O'Grady of the Kansas City Times will keep his pen off W. B. Harris, editor of the Smithville Democrat-Herald, next time. It happened like this when Steve wrote it up:
"This is from the 'School Notes' in the Smithville Democrat-Herald: 'Once more after a week's silence, Monday morning there pealed forth over the keen and frosty air the merry, inviting melodies of the school bell.' We'll bet teacher wrote that, won't you?"
But Harris looks at it this way:
"Guess again, brother. It was written by a member of the senior class, and teacher didn't see it until after it was printed. The melody of the school bell doesn't sound the same to everyone, you know."

W.B. thus continued to build on his success in the world of writing, editing, and advertising, and profited from his various connections and activities. He did not realize it at the time, but acquiring the *DH* would lead to significant advancements in his career. It would also instigate a series of events which would cause both peace and discord amidst the Blakes and the Mounts.

It started when he announced that he, Anna, and young Howard were moving their primary residence to Smithville. This meant the loss of the Mount family home in Higginsville, which was of sentimental value to Charles and Samantha Mount. They had moved there in the 1880s, and had raised the children there, including Anna, Edna, and Nona. Yet, they had now all set down roots in Kansas City. Charles and Samantha understood why Warren and Anna needed to relocate, and the family could still visit Higginsville at any time. They would indeed continue to make such visits to their old home, and to old friends like the Petersons.

The relocation also meant that Anna would not be in Kansas City as often. This came as no real concern or surprise—of course, Anna, Warren, and Howard would continue to travel between Smithville, Kansas City, St. Joseph, and neighboring areas frequently. They had always done so. It was par for the course in Warren's career. And yet, Nona was distraught by the prospect that she would not see her dear sister every day anymore. Indeed, during her pregnancy and in the months after Hurwitt's birth, Anna had visited daily and often spent several days at a time with her. It would not be the same, Nona argued. Would Anna now be able to travel the distance to Kansas City with baby Howard in tow? Would Nona be able to visit them, leaving Hurwitt in the care of her parents? It did not seem feasible.

Then, Warren did an incredible thing. He had an idea that would, as the saying goes, kill two birds with one stone. Nona wanted to stay close to Anna, and Nona also wanted to return to work in printing. The solution was clear. Warren proposed that Nona work as a printer for the *Smithville Democrat-Herald*. Everyone was present when he announced this proposal. Everyone except Charles Blake, who was at his parents' home on Troost Ave.

Nona accepted Warren's offer. In the same breath, Anna suggested that Nona stay with her and Warren for a week, maybe a little longer, to get her bearings and make a solid start at the *DH*. There was some discussion about Hurwitt. Nona preferred that he stay with her; Samantha Mount stated that he could be well looked-after by her.

It was in the midst of this back-and-forth that Charles Blake came through the door, looking tired and distraught. He had a tough day at the theatre. Production was slow, and roles were not easy to get. Having taken time away to look after Nona and the baby, Charles had lost several acting opportunities. It was unlikely that he would be able to continue in his chosen career. It was a sad truth, and one he had to accept. He had spoken with his father about the possibility of joining him in wholesale produce and grain. The idea was unappealing to Charles, but at least the income would support Nona and the child.

Charles was prepared to pull Nona into a private conversation, until he entered the house and saw the whole family—including Anna and W.B.—in their own deep discussion. They were talking about the baby, Hurwitt. Without bothering to say hello, Charles interjected with, "What's the matter with the baby? That's for me and Nona to discuss."

Everyone paused and looked up at him then, including Nona. Her eyes were bright, and she had an expression on her face that was familiar to him. He had seen it at times when she had made a decision about something.

She walked over to him and smiled softly. "Hello Charles. Baby is fine. But I have something to tell you." She grabbed his hand and continued, "I'm going back to work, like we talked about. I have a job in printing."

Charles gazed back at her in mild surprise. Unconsciously, he tugged his hand away. He did not want to have this conversation in front of them all, and yet here he was. "Well, that's real good, Nona. Real good. I have something to tell you too, but I'm not too glad about it." He decided to say it in a rush, to get it over with. "I'm done at the theatre, can't get work. So, I've been talking to my father about going into wholesale." He flicked his eyes to the others in the room; they were all looking at him. He stammered, "It's not set in stone yet."

As he said this, he could feel W.B. Harris' gaze from across the room. He could not look Harris in the eye, but he imagined that the gaze carried a lot of things within it: judgment, disapproval, righteousness. For the man was right. Charles had lost his job and now could not provide for Nona and the baby.

Nona was blinking at him, in a sad and sweet sort of way. When she spoke, it was oddly as if she had not heard what he had just said. "I've taken a position at the *Smithville Democrat-Herald*, Bernie's new paper. It's just for now, while I'm getting back on my feet. I'll take Hurwitt with me—he's still nursing, and he is just starting to bond with his cousin Howard…"

Nona realized too late that she had said too much too quickly. The look on Charles' face was unreadable. He was either furious or disinterested, and neither option was conducive to a family discussion. Anna swiftly intervened and suggested that Charles and Nona go into the bedroom to talk quietly. Without a word, they turned and walked away towards Nona's room, with the family silently watching them.

They remained in the room for just shy of an hour. When they joined everyone in the kitchen for dinner, everything was decided. Nona would travel with the Harrises to their home in Smithville and remain there for three weeks while commencing work at the *DH*. Meanwhile, Charles would continue living with his parents on Troost while he sorted out his next steps, whether that be acting or wholesale, or something else entirely. At the end of those three weeks, Charles and Nona were determined to both find secure employment in Kansas City. Nona thus agreed, as a compromise to Charles, that the *DH* would be a temporary, rather than a permanent, solution. Baby Hurwitt would remain with Nona—it was no question that the child should be with his mother.

The table was quiet as the couple shared these decisions. No one commented except for Warren, who scooped a spoonful of peas onto his plate and said, "So, business is looking up with Missouri auctioneers. But I did see a sale advertisement by the Gower Enterprise last week giving a General Dan Gibson as auctioneer."[2]

---

[2] *Kansas City Times*, February 8, 1913.

Anna smiled in a humoring sort of way and leaned towards her husband, sweeping her hand over his forearm. "I believe the Gower Enterprise could use your expertise in advertising, dear." She added, "And your charm and wit, Charles," turning her gaze to him.

But he sat stonily beside Nona, and thus, for the first time, Warren's joke fell on deaf ears.

The day of the departure for Smithville arrived quickly. Nona was sullen in the cold December days leading up to it, casting uncertain glances at her husband as he stood on the porch with his hands in his pockets and his head down. They had promised one another three weeks—three weeks to assuage the restlessness in their hearts before resuming their lives as a family in Kansas City. But, as Nona slipped into her brother-in-law's car with the baby, she was unsure whether it was the right decision to leave at all.

W.B. changed her perspective the minute they set forth for Smithville. He regaled her with stories about the paper and cheered everyone up by re-telling the story of how he had introduced his business partner, E.F. Livesay, to Ms. Edith Sebastian.

Back in the summer of 1912, the Harrises had a visit from Belle Mount-Sebastian (the older sister of Anna and Nona) and her husband, Richard M. Sebastian. The Sebastians had moved to Higginsville in the 1880s. Prior to that, the family resided in Hancock County, Ohio and McPherson County, Kansas. Belle Mount had married Richard Sebastian in 1891 and they had seven children together, four boys and two girls. Their eldest daughter, Edith, was eighteen years old and unmarried. She had worked under W.B at the *Jeffersonian* for some time.[3]

---

[3] 1910 US Federal Census Record for Belle Mount Sebastian, Lafayette, Higginsville, MO, listing: Richard M Sebastian (head, age 43); Belle Sebastian (wife, age 35); Charles Sebastian (son, age18); Edith M Sebastian (daughter, age 16); William G Sebastian (son, age 14); Elizabeth R Sebastian (daughter, age 11); Thelma C Sebastian (daughter, age 5); Richard A Sebastian (son, age 2). 1920 US Federal Census record includes youngest son Edwin B, who would be born about 1911.

Shortly after this visit, W.B. had travelled to Smithville on the urging of Lee Shippey to meet with E.F. Livesay. It was during this trip that W.B. and E.F. began negotiations over the future of the *Smithville Democrat-Herald*. The fruitfulness of their discussion, and the affable natures of both men, led to casual conversation about their respective families. W.B. proudly spoke of his wife and son and discerned that E.F. was still a bachelor. E.F. had admitted this a tad sheepishly and jokingly asked if W.B. knew of any eligible young women. At this, a twinkle appeared in W.B.'s eye and the wheels began turning. He invited E.F. to join him and Anna for lunch in Higginsville the following week.

The lunch indeed took place at the Harris residence. W.B. invited his niece, Edith Sebastian, to join them. Edith anticipated a normal visit with her aunt and uncle and was surprised to meet E.F. Livesay at the house. W.B. introduced him as a newspaper man and a business partner, and was prepared to stir up more conversation, but there was no need.

E.F. and Edith were drawn to each other from the moment their paths crossed. They cast curious glances at each other from across the table during lunch, and then walked together to converse outside. By the end of the afternoon, it was clear to both W.B. and Anna that they were quite smitten. This was confirmed when Anna heard E.F. ask Edith if he could see her again.

Within several months, Belle Mount-Sebastian told Anna that E.F. Livesay had proposed marriage to her daughter Edith. When Anna shared this with W.B., he laughed aloud.

"I suppose you think you're quite the matchmaker now?" Anna had murmured, looking amused and irritated.

Still laughing, W.B. replied, "They'll be married by the year's end, mark my words." He stood up from his seat at the table and closed the draft issue of the *Jeffersonian* he had been editing. There was a gleam in his eyes as he drew closer to Anna and said, "I wager a December wedding—a Christmastime wedding—would be just right, don't you think?"

Anna sighed wistfully, allowing him to slip his arm about her waist and kiss her softly. It was clear that he was referring to their own December wedding, and the pleasant memories it roused. "If the wedding were to be just like ours," she whispered, "Then yes. It would be just right."

W.B. and Anna had married on December 12, 1908. Edwin F. Livesay and Edith M. Sebastian were married on December 21, 1912. A Christmastime wedding, indeed. It was a small and intimate ceremony held at home in Higginsville and attended by the parents on both sides (Edwin's living parent, William Livesay, and Edith's parents, Richard Sebastian and Belle Mount).[4] W.B., Anna, and Nona attended. It was a beautiful and lovely occasion to unite the families and further solidify the friendship and business partnership between W.B. and E.F.

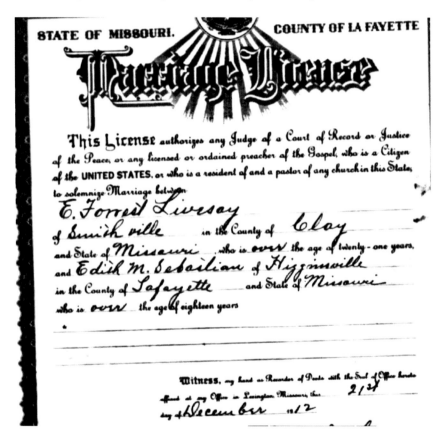

Marriage license issued to E. Forrest Livesay and Edith M. Sebastian, Lafayette County, MO, Dec. 21, 1912.

---

[4] See US Federal Census record for 1910 for Richard and Belle Sebastian; and US Federal Census record for 1900 for William F. Livesay, listing the Livesay family residing in Lafayette Co, MO (William F Levasy, age 42, Head; Alice A Fishback-Levasy, age 41, Wife; Wayne Levasy, age 13, Son; Forrest Levasy, age 10, Son; Lillian Levasy, age 8, Daughter; Rebekkah Levasy, age 4, Daughter; Annie Levasy, age 1, Daughter). Alice Fishback passed away in 1904.

Marriage Licenses.

Marriage licenses have been issued to:

W. C. Davis .. .. .. Aullville
Glenna S. Burrow .. Concordia

E. Forrest Livesay ..Smithville
Edith M. Sebastian ..Higginsville

Mr. and Mrs. Forest Livesay, of Smithville, Mo. arrived Thursday for a brief visit in Marshall, the guests of the formers aunt, Mrs. C. A. Prather, and his two sisters, Misses Lillian and Rebecca Livesay. Mr. Livesay is one of the owners of the Smithville Herald.

<u>Right</u>: *The Lexington Intelligencer,* Dec. 27, 1912; <u>Left</u>: *Saline County Weekly Progress,* Dec. 27, 1912.

"We are all family now, you see?" W.B. stated, as he concluded the story. He glanced over at Nona, who was seated in the back seat of the Model-T with Hurwitt in her lap. She was smiling and nodding in agreement.

"How nice it is. And how exciting that you will be working at Bernie's and Forrest's paper," Anna remarked. She was seated beside W.B. in the front, with Howard in her arms. She turned her head to give Nona a reassuring smile.

"I am excited about it," Nona replied, and bent down to kiss Hurwitt, who began to coo and fuss. "And maybe it doesn't need to be temporary. Maybe..." She paused, allowing the train of thought to fade away. She had been wondering what would have happened if Charles had decided to join them. Could they not have all made a life in Smithville—she, Charles, and Hurwitt; Anna, Bernie, and Howard; Forrest and Edith? But it was too late to second-guess, too late to think about that now. They had made their beds and now must lie in them.

Bernie and Forrest were a force to be reckoned with and were eager to reinvigorate the paper. Before they could get down to serious work, however, they had to contend with the quips and ribbing from their colleagues about Forrest's recent marriage to Miss Edith Sebastian. Of course, this news spread throughout the entire state of Missouri within hours of the ink being dry on the marriage license.

The *Jeffersonian's* Lee Shippey was the first to hear about it outside of the Harris-Mount-Sebastian families, and true to form, he penned a story and shared his commentary with colleagues at the *Kansas City Times.* In retrospect, Shippey regretted sharing his thoughts with one particular *Times* writer who decided to take some creative liberties. The article published in the January 6, 1913 issue of the *Times* bore the headline, "Stole Lee Shippey's Treasure." When W.B. Harris read this, he laughed at the clever play on words and was determined to congratulate the writer at the *Times,* and give Shippey a hard time about losing Edith to Forrest:

STOLE LEE SHIPPEY'S TREASURE.

"Miss Edith Sebastian, a valued employee of the Jeffersonian, and Forrest Livesay, one of the owners of the Smithville Democrat-Herald, were married December 21," writes Lee Shippey. "They went to Smithville the last of last week. We think a whole lot of both of them and have given them our forgiveness. But we are rigging up a guillotine over our threshold, and the next time a young man comes along trying to steal our treasures, we are going to press the button."

Once all the ribbing and comments were out of the men's systems (for the time being, anyway), Bernie and Forrest set to work. The *Smithville Democrat-Herald* would be a weekly, sixteen-page paper with articles of relevance to Clay County locals. Bernie would pen his own editorials and have a hands-on role as editor. Forrest would manage production and distribution. Their office would employ several printers, binders, and compositors, including Nona.

The month of January was extremely busy as they worked to publish these initial issues and establish a new and efficient workflow. Nona was just as committed to the paper's success as everyone else. Before she realized it, three weeks had turned into four, and four weeks had turned into eight. She wrote home to her husband, Charles, frequently, telling him about Smithville, her work, and about how baby Hurwitt was doing. After she had been in Smithville four weeks, she wrote again, asking if he would be terribly upset if she extended her visit. His reply was short; in it, he assured her that she could stay in Smithville if she desired, as long as she and Hurwitt were doing well. He also wrote that he had not found secure employment yet.[5] He estimated that he would have a stable situation within the next three weeks. Nona found this curious but did not think about it too much. She and Hurwitt were quite happy in Smithville, and if Charles needed more time, then she would give it to him.

Nona thus remained in Smithville at the Harris home. She enjoyed her work at the paper and loved spending time with her family. It was an utter joy to see the children, Frank Hurwitt Blake and Howard Bernard Harris, happy and growing together, and she had ample opportunities to spend time with her cousin, Edith. The Livesays were a fine family, and Forrest treated Edith like a queen. How lucky, Nona had thought, as she watched these two well-matched couples: Anna and Bernie; Edith and Forrest. *Charles and I will be like that one day,* she told herself. *Just as soon as he gets settled, we will be just as happy.*

---

[5] US City Directory for 1912, Kansas City, MO, lists Charles A. Blake working as roofer for Banner Roofing Company and residing at 1327 Lydia Ave. The same directory lists James H. Blake (Blake & Kelley) residing at 1418 Virginia Ave. These were all adjacent streets and both the Mounts and Blakes moved around this residential area. It appears that Charles thus obtained temporary work as a roofer in 1912. There is no directory listing for James H. Blake or Charles A. Blake in Kansas City, MO in 1913.

The time for her to find out arrived in March. Bernie had said that, as much as he wished her to continue at the paper, she must go home to her husband and her parents. When Nona protested, Bernie reminded her that he and Anna had encouraged Charles Blake to join them in Smithville. He had even offered to find Charles a job in printing if he wanted. All of these offers were rejected. Charles' last letter entreated Nona to come home. Apparently, he had found secure employment. He stated that he had a duty to provide for his wife and child, and that he would now live up to that duty. He closed the letter by stating that he would come collect Nona and Hurwitt if Bernie could not drive them home and to please "make arrangements as soon as possible so we can start our lives."

W.B. did not like the tone of this letter. He did not take kindly to the intimation that he was somehow keeping Nona away from her Kansas City family. Furthermore, Charles Blake seemed to imply that their lives—his and Nona's—were separate from the rest of the family. This bothered W.B. more than the rest of the letter. The Mounts, the Blakes, the Harrises, and now the Sebastians and the Livesays, were all part of the same, integrated family. What on earth could Charles be getting at? No, something was not quite right.

W.B. drove Nona and Hurwitt back to Kansas City in late March 1913. Anna remained in Smithville with their son Howard. Forrest and Edith would manage the paper during W.B.'s absence.

When they arrived home to Harrison Ave., they expected a warm homecoming from Nona's parents, and indeed received one. However, as the afternoon passed, Nona told W.B. and her parents that she ought to reunite with Charles at his parents' home on Troost. There was nothing wrong with this, and Nona was perfectly capable of traveling the swift block to Troost with Hurwitt. Still, W.B. offered—in fact, insisted—to escort them.

When they arrived at the Blake home, all was calm, and Charles Blake greeted Nona and Hurwitt with affection. As W.B. stood watching this exchange, he was reassured, and he told himself that he had imagined the odd tone in Charles' letter.

But then, something happened that would confirm his perception of Charles and alter the course of their lives.

CHAPTER 5

Charles Blake encouraged Nona to come inside with Frank Hurwitt, insisting that they must be tired from the journey. W.B. began to follow them in, but Charles stood in the doorway as if to refuse him entry. W.B. narrowed his eyes.

"I need a private word with Nona," Charles muttered in a quiet and steely voice. "She doesn't need you anymore, none of you."

W.B. clenched his hands in his pockets and his chest expanded. This alone was enough to make Charles shrink back. W.B., still so strong and finely built, could have easily swatted away Charles' thin frame. Instead, he remained standing there, as if intending to wear down Charles by the strength of his presence. After a few tense moments, he muttered, "Say that again, why don't you? And this time, within earshot of Nona."

There was a menacing edge to his voice, and he had spoken loudly enough for Nona to in fact hear him. Charles was faltering, his attempt to block the door feeble. Before he could respond, Nona was there, balancing Frank Hurwitt against her hip and looking concerned.

"What are you two talking about—nothing serious? Come on inside then, and Bernie will tell you all about his paper while we wait for your parents, Charles."

Charles stepped back, looking somewhat defeated but unable to push back against Nona's entreating face and W.B.'s imposing stature. W.B. easily slipped by him and followed Nona into the living room as she began telling him how glad she was that he had come with her. He could tell Charles about her work at the *Smithville Democrat-Herald* much better than she could, and how fine a paper it was, she boasted. W.B. smiled, watching her as she settled young Hurwitt into the chair beside her, and replied, "Yes, I'm sure Charles, and Mr. and Mrs. Blake, will be pleased to hear about it. But it sounds like Charles has something to discuss with you."

It was at that moment that Charles entered the room. Perhaps he had been waiting, hovering at the front door to decide how to speak with Nona. Charles knew she had certain expectations of what their lives would be like in Kansas City. He also knew that what he was about to share would shatter those expectations.

Charles watched W.B. kneel to hug and kiss Hurwitt, and then lean towards Nona. "Do you wish me to leave so that you and Charles can talk alone?"

"Of course not," she replied. Her eyes grew big, and she stood up to walk over to Charles, taking his hand to pull him into a chair. "Whatever it is, we can talk about it together," she urged. "We're family."

Charles sat with his hands on his knees, his gaze shifting from Nona to W.B. At length, he cleared his throat, and muttered, "My parents. They won't be coming back to join us. They've already left, two days ago."

"They've left?" Nona inquired. "And what do you mean about them not coming back?" A look of distress flashed across her face.

Charles noticed it, and his tone softened. "Oh, they are completely all right. No need to worry. They boarded the train, bound for California. My father secured a position at the docks, in a city called San Pedro."

This does not assuage Nona; if anything, it increased her distress. "Your parents left to go all the way to California? But your father—he had such a good job here. Why on earth did they leave? And why did you not tell me about this before, in your letter?"

W.B. leaned forward in his seat, glad to hear Nona speak the words that were on his mind. He too wondered why Charles had not bothered to write about this in his numerous letters to Nona. Surely, a significant move such as this would have taken weeks of planning and preparation.

"But that's what I've been trying to tell you. That's why I wanted you to come home, to talk to you about it," Charles responded.

His pleading tone did not have its intended effect on Nona. She sat back in her chair, her arms folded, and her lips pouted. "I certainly would have liked to know about this before, instead of coming home to find them gone. And they didn't even stay to say goodbye to me, and more importantly, to Hurwitt." A crack sounded in her voice and her eyes became damp. "I thought your parents cared about us."

Charles stood up, as if to approach her, but W.B. stood as well, effectively halting him in his steps. "Is that all?" he asked, turning to stare at Charles harshly.

Charles visibly swallowed. "No." He looked past W.B. towards his wife, but her eyes were drawn down. The next words he spoke came out in a rush as he desperately tried to appeal to Nona while avoiding W.B.'s stare. "There was no need for my parents to say goodbye, because…well, because I've got a position too, out in San Pedro. The fishing business is real lucrative. We discussed it, my parents and I, and I figure that we can make a nice life out there in California. We don't need to be here anymore, see? We'll join them and then we'll all be together, Nona. We could board the train tomorrow, next week, whenever you're ready."

Nona started crying then, and that's what did it. W.B. had kept cool and calm for her sake, but when he heard her distress and saw her tears, he could no longer restrain himself. Within a flash, he yanked Charles away from Nona and pinned him against the wall.

"How dare you make these plans without consulting with your wife, without consulting with her family," he breathed, his face inches away from Charles. "Family means everything to Nona, to me, to every one of the Mounts. And yet you didn't bother to mention this in your letters? Didn't bother to discuss this properly with the family?" He loosened his grip on Charles' arm only slightly to glance back at Nona. She was rocking the child and tears still brimmed from her eyes.

"No, I didn't." Charles voice was shaky, and his eyes bore an obstinate glint. "She is my wife. Where I go, she will follow, whether I've discussed it with you all or not. You've no right to interfere."

W.B. felt the fire build within him and he was prepared to deliver a blow that would catapult Charles through the house and clear across the street. Nona's desperate yell stopped him. He exercised the utmost restraint to release Charles and step back.

Nothing else, besides his own wife's interference, could have prevented him from striking Charles that day. He did not do or say anything more. It was Nona who held the baby tightly to her chest and begged W.B. to take her back home. She would not look directly at W.B. or Charles.

Homeward they went, leaving Charles alone in the Blake house. But it was not over. It was far from over.

In retrospect, Charles realized that he could have handled things better. He also realized, perhaps a little too late, that it was unwise to cross Warren B. Harris. Charles had underestimated the man before, thinking him vain and arrogant. The truth of it was, however, that Warren B. Harris was a prominent newspaper man with connections to other prominent, politically powerful people. The truth of it was that Warren B. Harris only needed to place a simple call to make good on his promise to run Charles out of town.

Over that next week, Nona and Hurwitt remained in the protective embrace of the Mounts. The Mount patriarch did not say much after W.B. gave a brief account of what had transpired at the Blake house. Mr. Charles Mount did say, however, that he was disappointed in his son-in-law's approach to the matter. Furthermore, he was disappointed in the lack of communication from James and Ada Blake.

Glass plate negative taken by A.T. Peterson of Charles S. Mount and Samantha Carrol Mount, c. 1917

Portrait of the family of Charles T. Blake, the grandfather of Charles A. Blake. James H. Blake is in the back row, the second on the right.

He admitted to W.B. that James Blake had talked casually about the job opportunities at the California docks in fishing and operating boats. Apparently, the southern California cities of San Pedro and Redondo Beach were rich in fish like abalone, sardines, and anchovies, which could be harvested at a great profit. These and other types of marine specimens were high in demand as food sources. Rumor had it that a man who could secure work in the fishing industry in California would make a good living for himself.[1]

Still, he agreed that the Blakes should have discussed their plans with the entire family and was thankful to W.B. for bringing his daughter and grandson back home.

---

[1] San Pedro, CA has a rich history as a fishing and marine community, and workers in the fishing industry could make a good living. See, e.g., a recent documentary "The Smell of Money: The Story of the Fishing and Canning Industry of the Los Angeles Harbor Area" (2024), with interviews of San Pedro families who attest, "everyone who worked in the fishing industry...there was not a poor person around...it was the smell of money." See also historical text on the fishing industry in CA, 1900-1913: California State Fisheries Laboratory, et. al., *The Scientific Investigation of Marine Fisheries: As Related to the Work of the Fish and Game Commission in Southern California, Volumes 1-11* (California State Printing Office, Jan. 1913).

"We will talk to Charles later this week once everyone has cooled off," Mr. Mount said firmly. "My mother always said that no discussions can be had when folks are upset." A nostalgic look passed across his face, and he shook his head to clear it. "Now then," he resumed, looking at W.B. with interest. "What are you going to do? Have you written to Annie?"

"I have, yes," W.B. responded, smiling slightly at the term of endearment Mr. Mount had used for his older daughter. "And I plan to go on back to Smithville, but not until I'm sure things are settled here." He looked at Mr. Mount with intent, his eyes communicating more than mere words could.

The two men were silent for a few moments, listening to the sounds of Nona and Mrs. Mount bustling about in the back of the house. Then, very slowly, Mr. Mount looked W.B. steadily in the eye and said, "You do what you have to do to keep our Nonie home."

W.B.'s first outing was to the offices of the *Kansas City Star*. His friends would be there, and if he was lucky, so would the paper's proprietor, Bill Nelson. Fortune found him that day: he was granted a meeting with Nelson, shared a cigar with two of the staff editors, and was given leeway to place a telephone call.

The Kansas City Star offices, located at 11th and Grand Ave, Kansas City. Source: William Rockhill Nelson, The Story of a Man, a Newspaper and a City, p. 60.

He dialed the *Smithville Democrat-Herald* straight away. Forrest answered, and W.B. launched into the purpose of his call without preliminaries. They spoke for several minutes, and then W.B. heard a female in the background. There was a rustle, and then Anna's voice came on the line. He felt a ripple of relief wash over him as soon as he heard it.

"Annie, I'm at the *Star*," he began, and, as concisely as possible, he conveyed Mr. Charles Mount's directive. "I'll be home as soon as it's done," he promised. Anna urged him to be careful and assured him that all was in order at the *DH*. "Love you, from me and Howard," she murmured before the line grew quiet.

Before leaving the *Star* office, W.B. promised to return with a box of tobacco the next time he was in the vicinity. Nelson shook his hand on this and muttered, "Don't mention it, Bern." He patted W.B. on the shoulder before easing his large and imposing frame into his armchair.

On the drive back to the residential area of Kansas City, W.B. was followed by two men driving separately in their clean, 1913 Ford Model-Ts. W.B. glanced over at them occasionally, offering a discreet nod. He pulled onto Troost Avenue; the other cars parked a block away on Forrest Avenue. The men sat quietly in their cars, watching and waiting. Within just over a half-hour, Charles A. Blake made his appearance. W.B. watched him exit the house and fiddle with his keys as he stood on the front porch. When he finally turned to walk down the street, W.B. exited his car.

A look of surprise crossed over Charles' face, and he approached W.B. with interest. This was enough to keep W.B. cool and level-headed. This was an opportunity to see if Charles had changed his mind. At the least, W.B. could determine if Charles has seriously thought about the consequences of what he had proposed to Nona.

"Warren," Charles greeted, with a slight edge to his tone. He had never referred to his brother-in-law as "W.B." or "Bernie." It was always "Warren."

"Where are Nona and Hurwitt, aren't they with you? I've been coming by the house, but Nona won't see me. Mr. Mount won't even admit me in."

W.B. uttered a harsh sigh. "Well, do you blame him? You're proposing to take away his daughter."

"He's keeping me from my wife and child," Charles retorted, a flash of anger appearing in his eyes.

W.B. caught the anger in his expression, and the fact that Charles had raised his voice. And he knew that he would need to follow through with what he planned and arranged. "Charles, I'm going to say this only once. There are two basic choices here. I'm giving you the rare opportunity to make the right choice, so listen closely. Choice one: you can stay here, get a legitimate job in the city, and man up to be the husband and father you should be. You can move in with Nona and the boy, where Mr. and Mrs. Mount will support you." He paused for a moment, allowing this to sink in. "Choice two: you get the hell out of town and never come back."

W.B. stared hard at Charles, as if daring him to contradict him or argue. Charles took the bait. "I don't choose either. Nona is my wife, and Hurwitt is my child, damn it! They'll be coming to California with me."

Even as he said this, Charles somehow knew he would regret it. He somehow knew that he was out of bargaining power and that he might never see Nona and Hurwitt again.

W.B. strolled closer to Charles, letting out a low whistle. "Remember, back when little Frank Hurwitt was born and we had a nice conversation, just the two of us? If memory serves, I believe I said that if you can't be a good husband and father, then I'd run you out of town faster than you can blink."

Charles' mouth grew dry, and he could not respond. He blinked.

Charles A. Blake had vanished from Kansas City.

On April 8, 1913, W.B. Harris escorted Nona L. Mount-Blake to the courthouse in Independence, Missouri to file for divorce against Charles A. Blake. The court could not locate Blake within the state of Missouri and the suit was dropped for lack of venue, meaning that the state could not exercise jurisdiction over both parties.

When questions began to arise about Charles Blake, and rumors began to swirl, W.B. put a halt to them immediately. He spread the word that Nona's husband, Charles A. Blake, was dead and that Nona was a widow.

The Mount-Harris families accepted this as true and did their best to move on with their lives. Nona secured a position at a Kansas City printing company and carried herself as a widow and a single mother. She rented a room on her own for a while, but eventually moved back in with her parents.

The city directory for Kansas City, Missouri, 1913, lists Nona Blake working as a clerk and residing at 1522 Troost Avenue.

And the city directory for San Diego, California, 1913, lists Chas. A. Blake residing at 1144 Grape Street.

Two Divorce Suits at County Seat.
These suits for divorce were brought in Independence yesterday: Nona L. against Charles A. Blake, Flora D. against John Kolster.

Kansas City Times, April 9, 1913.

Editorial in the Kansas City Times, *January 11, 1913, "Hide the Divorce Causes: Real Reasons Seldom Heard in Court, the Proctor Says."*

MANY ELOPEMENTS END BADLY.
"Rarely is there a divorce when the man and woman marry after they have reached a mature age and have not been divorced before. Most divorces are granted to women who are married when they are young—eloped to another state and married—and didn't find the married life as they expected. Young women are not educated to understand the domestic relations. Men are not educated to appreciate women in the right way and to select a wife by the standard of worth. A pretty face and a smile will cause some men to lose sight of everything else. The smile isn't always there in future years and the beauty begins to fade. Then things break. The divorce court is the next step.

CHAPTER 6

May 1913-December 1913
Kansas City & Smithville, Missouri

Life proceeded as normally as expected for Nona Mount-Blake following her separation from Charles A. Blake. In the eyes of the public, and in the eyes of her family members (namely, Warren B. Harris), Charles was deceased, and Nona was widow. This characterization won her the sympathy of other ladies in town, who offered their condolences and who expressed pity that little Frank Hurwitt had lost his father at such a young age. "To grow up without a father…such a shame. You will stay home and raise him, of course," the ladies said to Nona. And Nona was patient and accepted being cast as the pitiful young widow for a while. But the act soon wore thin.

She remained outwardly demure and cordial, but her heart and mind were chaotic. She knew that Charles was not dead. She could not prove it, and the family refused to discuss it, but she knew that Charles was somewhere in California. They had planned a life together, and that was all stripped away by W.B. Harris. Nona knew that W.B., and maybe Anna too, had been responsible for Charles' disappearance. This engendered discordant feelings within her. She loved her sister and brother-in-law dearly, but they really had never given Charles a chance. Did Nona wish to leave her Missouri family and move to California? She had not been given the time and space to decide. And she had been so upset with the entire situation that she had agreed to file for divorce against Charles. Her father, W.B., and Anna had been her sounding board and had helped her make the decision. Or had they made the decision for her?

She was unsure and she was stuck. Charles had been effectively declared dead, and Nona was living with her parents under that guise of widowhood. She had no choice but to pick up where she left off, slowly taking up work as a clerk in a printing office while her parents helped care for Frank Hurwitt.

W.B. Harris, meanwhile, returned to Smithville to resume work at the paper. He had offered Nona a permanent position as a printer, but she declined. For reasons she could not fully articulate, she needed time apart from W.B. and Anna. This meant that their sons—Frank Hurwitt Blake and Howard Bernard Harris—would be separated and would likely not grow up together as they had originally planned. But she could not turn back now. The damage was done.

What is right? Was any of it up to her, or had she been forced to forge a path chosen by others? Nona would never be able to answer these questions during her lifetime.

She convinced herself that she was better off without Charles and was determined to make a career in the printing industry without W.B.'s interference. And thus, she moved on.

W.B. Harris had no qualms about what transpired in April 1913. To the contrary, he was relieved to be rid of the problem and eager to return to his life and duties in Smithville. And, when he returned, he was so busy with the paper and his various social engagements that he simply could not spare a single thought for Charles A. Blake.

The *Smithville Democrat-Herald* increased its readership tenfold during the first six months of 1913. By the fall, the office was fully staffed and generating more profits than it had in the past five years. There was a slight hiccup in staffing in May, but that was due to the marriage of several female employees. W.B.'s newspaper friends in Marshall, Missouri caught wind of this, and felt compelled to give him a hard time, and give Lee Shippey a ribbing for good measure.[1]

---

[1] *The Marshall Republican,* "Round About," May 23, 1913.

By that time, Shippey had become nationally known as a "poet-philosopher" and frequent speaker at conferences and meetings of the Press Association. On August 9, 1913, Shippey would be a speaker at the Clinton, Missouri Chautauqua, a popular eight-day event filled with music, entertainment, and educational lectures.[2]

The Chautauqua had originated in the 1870s as an educational experiment to promote secular adult education and lifelong learning. By the early 1900s, "circuit Chautauquas" became popular, whereby individual cities contracted to hold three-to-eight-day educational programs of lectures, music, dramatic readings, and entertainment. Cities throughout the state of Missouri held their own Chautauquas, and booked prominent speakers and performers, including Lee Shippey, Secretary of State William Jennings Bryan, and Vice President of the United States Thomas R. Marshall.[3]

All Missouri papers would cover the yearly Chautauqua, including the *Smithville Democrat-Herald*, which would joke that "many people have been puzzled over the proper pronunciation...Higginsville...decided to call it 'Chat-ti-Kway' but Platte City...called it 'Show-talk-away,' which perhaps covers the meaning more clearly."[4]

[2] *The Henry County Republican*, "Lee Shippey at Chautauqua," July 31, 1913; *The Concordian*, April 30, 1914: "Lee Shippey, the editor of the Higginsville Jeffersonian, attended the National Press Association meeting at Dallas, Texas, and was one of the speakers. Thus he has become a national person and all who know him are glad about it."

[3] Gina Misiroglu, "Chautauqu Movement" in *American Countercultures: An Encyclopedia of Nonconformists, Alternative Lifestyles, and Radical Ideas in U.S. History* (Routledge, 2015): 133-34; The 1913 MO Chautauqua booked Sec. Bryan, and the 1914 event booked V.P. Marshall (see programs in e.g., *The Henry County Republican*, July 24, 1913, and *The La Belle Star*, August 14, 1914). See also University of Iowa's digital collection, "Traveling Culture: Circuit Chautauqua in the Twentieth Century" at digital.lib.uiowa.edu/tc/

[4] The *Smithville Democrat-Herald*, quoted in the *King City Democrat*, September 4, 1914.

LEE SHIPPEY TO SPEAK HERE

Poet-Philosopher of Higginsville to Address Chautauqua Audience.

Lee Shippey, the poet-philosopher of Higginsville and the editor of the Jeffersonian, is to speak here during the Chautauqua, August 24-31. He is well known here, having appeared on Journalism Week programs in past years.

Mr. Shippey began his career as a journalist by reading proof on the Kansas City Star. Later he was in charge of a column of humor called "The Tidings of the Times," in the Kansas City Times. He was sent by that paper to cover the state press association meetings, and there became interested in country journalism. When the editor of the Higginsville Jeffersonian died, Mr. Shippey bought that paper.

Every Sunday he has a column of verse in the Kansas City Star.

LEE SHIPPEY AT CHAUTAUQUA.

There is a good deal of interest among Clinton people as to the coming of Lee Shippey, editor of the Higginsville Jeffersonian, who will appear at the Clinton Chautauqua this year. Mr. Shippey is one of the best known newspaper men in the state, and was for years on the Kansas City Star, the Missouri Notes being among his work on that paper. Since buying the Jeffersonian a few years ago, Mr. Shippey has been a regular contributor to the Sunday Star, his work being mainly of a humorous nature. Many readers of THE REPUBLICAN remember his "Jests in Jingle" and will be glad to listen to his platform lecture.

Columbia Missourian, Aug. 8, 1913;
Henry County Republican, July 31, 1913

ROUND ABOUT •

It strange how some people must swallow a dose of their own medicine occasionally and in the meantime it has come home to them double strength. A few months ago our friend, W. B. Harris, foreman of the Higginsville Jeffersonian, bought the Smithville Democrat-Herald and on leaving his position took one of the two lady compositors with him as a bride. At Smithville Mr. Harris employed two lady compositors and last week one left him to get married and the other is going the same way soon, leaving him in worse shape than he left Editor Shippey, and Mr. Shippey is now doing some tall crowing.

Marshall Republican,
May 23, 1913, referring to W.B. Harris' marriage to Anna Mount when both were employed at the Jeffersonian. The writer is teasing Harris & Shippey.
Above, portrait of Harris, c. 1912.

Glass plate negatives of Lee Shippey, taken by A.T. Peterson, 1910s. Shippey was also a columnist for the Kansas City Star and served in France during WWI. He moved to Los Angeles, CA in 1920 after a highly publicized and scandalous divorce from his wife. While in France, he became romantically involved with another woman. After divorcing his first wife, he married the other woman, moved to LA, and became a prominent writer for the LA Times.

All of the talk about the upcoming Chautauqua was thus big news for Mr. Shippey and his comrades, but that was not the only news that arrived in the Spring of 1913. When W.B. Harris returned to Smithville after bringing Nona to Kansas City and dealing with the aftermath, he had a discussion with his partner, E.F. Livesay.

Forrest updated him on the plans and projections for the paper and advised him of a family matter: he and his wife, Edith, were expecting their first child. W.B. was thrilled and congratulated him, extolling the virtues of fatherhood. Forrest was in full agreement with these sentiments, though also shared some misgivings. He expressed some concern about Edith, and a desire that she should be near family. His father, William Livesay, still resided in Higginsville, as did Edith's parents, Richard and Belle Mount-Sebastian. Edith missed her mother, and wanted her help when the time came for the baby to arrive. Forrest stated that he and Edith would likely take some trips to Higginsville but assured W.B. that he would remain as committed as ever to the paper. W.B. did not doubt his friend and business partner in the least, and they proceeded as planned with ensuring the paper's success.

Things began to change, however, in the fall. By September, Edith Livesay was indisposed and unable to contribute to the paper. Forrest grew increasingly concerned for her health, and the health of the baby. A doctor attended her and recommended bedrest. The doctor advised that, should she wish to travel to family, she must make arrangements as soon as possible.

In light of this, Forrest felt it imperative that he travel with Edith to her parents' home in Higginsville. W.B. was understanding of this and encouraged it.

"The *D.H.* will be in good hands until you return, Anna and I will see to it," W.B. promised, and asked Forrest to give him a call once he and Edith were settled.

Forrest did call W.B. while in Higginsville from the *Jeffersonian* offices, about a week after he and Edith had arrived at the Sebastian home. "Bernie, I'm at the *Jeffersonian*. Lee gives his best regards."

W.B. let out a soft laugh. "Of course, Lee waited a mere hour after you arrived before asking you to pay a visit. What's he trying to do—steal my business partner?"

At this remark, Forrest became oddly quiet for a moment. "Bern, Edith's at home with her parents now and needs rest. The baby could arrive in a matter of weeks. She needs to stay here in Higginsville until the birth, and probably for a good while after. I…well, I need to stay here too."

"Well, sure Forrest, you have to," W.B. breathed. "You're a good husband and you'll be a good father. Stay as long as you need. I'll manage the *D.H.* and keep you informed until you come back in full capacity. In the meantime, you can draft the editorials and send…"

Forrest sighed deeply. "That's just it. Of course, you can manage the *D.H.* and you've done a damn good job. You're a newspaper man through and through and could give anyone a run for their money, even Lee. But so am I, Bern. I've got to be where the action is, and right now, with Edith…well, I've got to be in Higginsville." There was a pause, the line grew quiet, and W.B. had an odd foreboding of what was to come. "I've talked with Lee," Forrest resumed, "And he's offered a place for me at the *Jeffersonian.*"[5]

This revelation was not a complete surprise to W.B.—men in the newspaper business moved from one establishment to another all the time—but it still hit him hard. Forrest was more than co-owner of the *D.H.* He was a friend. He was family. "You're going to take it, then," W.B. responded, his voice heavy.

"I think I have to, Bern. And I want to leave the *D.H.* to you."

"We can discuss the details later," W.B. replied, the heaviness like a weight in his chest. "Give my best to Edith and everyone."

---

[5] E.F. Livesay did work for the *Jeffersonian* for some time while residing in Higginsville. His draft registration card for WWI, date June 5, 1917, lists his residence as Higginsville and his employer as the *Higginsville Jeffersonian.* Eventually, he and Edith would move to Kansas City and he would work for many years as a printer for Breeders Printing Company. See city directories for Kansas City for E Forrest Livesay, 1914 through 1924.

In late September, it was done. Forrest drove up to Smithville to finalize the sale of his interest in the *D.H.* to W.B. The transaction was printed in the *Times*:

> W. B. Harris of the Smithville Democrat-Herald has bought the interest of E. F. Livesay, his partner. The Democrat-Herald is always bright and readable; Mr. Harris has a keen eye and a sharp pair of shears, and if a credit line is mislaid occasionally, why, not many people besides the editor and the man who wrote the piece notice it.

Kansas City Times,
Oct. 6, 1913.

In November 1913, W.B. paid a visit to the Livesays and dropped by the *Jeffersonian*. All was well and everyone was in good spirits. The Livesay baby had not yet arrived, but Belle Mount-Sebastian was confident the child would be born soon and in good health. Edith was well and under Belle's dutiful care.

W.B. also dropped by the *Kansas City Star*. It was time he made good on his promise to bring the staff a box of the best tobacco he could find. He did just that, and they had a grand old time that afternoon.

W. B. Harris, editor of the Smithville Democrat-Herald, was in the sanctum yesterday morning with a bunch of the fine old tobacco raised only four blocks from the Smithville postoffice. He had a bunch of the 1911 crop of selected white burley which topped the Kentucky tobacco market. We smoked some of it in our trusty hod and it was some smoke, believe us! The 1913 crop was smaller on account of the drought, but its quality was not impaired. "The smile of some people is like a ray of sunshine and the frown of others is like a thunder cloud. Far better to smile and give cheer than to frown and cause unpleasantness," Colonel Harris wrote in the last issue of his paper, and he is the kind who smiles and brings cheer. Come again, Mr. Harris, we are glad to see you any time.

Kansas City Times,
Nov. 28, 1913

The news they had all been waiting for finally arrived a week later. Forrest and Edith's child was born on December 5, 1913. It was a little girl whom they christened "Leta Belle." The child was indeed born strong and healthy, and Belle was the proudest and most loving grandmother. Edith's bond to her mother grew even stronger, and she was glad of her decision to return home. There was something unique about the bond between the Mount women through the generations. In time, they always came back to one another, helping one another through thick and thin.

The Mount-Harris-Sebastian-Livesay families had their fair share of sorrow and difficulties in 1913. And yet, with the birth of baby Leta Belle in December, there was a glimmer of joy again and a reminder of the families' resilience.

Portrait of Richard M. Sebastian and wife Belle Mount-Sebastian, c. 1916

Leta Belle Livesay, 1931. Photo in East High School Yearbook, Kansas City. The quote underneath her photo reads, "The warmth of her heart exceeds that of her hair."

Left: Edna Mount (Belle's sister), center: Belle Mount, and far right is Belle's daughter Edith. c. 1942

CHAPTER 7

1914-1915
Los Angeles, California

When Charles A. Blake left Missouri in 1913, he knew he could never return. He arrived in San Diego, California in April, and from there travelled to Hermosa Beach to join his parents and siblings.

James H. Blake secured a position in wholesale meat packing with the Morris Packing Company, a large and profitable enterprise. The company had offices in several states including Missouri, Illinois, Nebraska, and California. The entire family—Mrs. Ada Blake, daughter Hattie, and son Theodore—had travelled with James to Hermosa Beach to make a new life. James H. Blake ("J.H.") made a decent living in the wholesale industry, but he was keenly interested in what the fishing industry had to offer.

The fisheries and canneries were a significant and extremely profitable industry along the California coast, primarily in the cities of San Francisco, San Diego, and San Pedro. The mid-to-late 1800s gave rise to an expansion of fisheries along the California coast. At the time, substantial immigration to southern California created a new market for fishery products, and both San Pedro and San Diego began to be important ports. The canneries developed rapidly, with high profit margins, due to increased demand for sardines, tuna, and albacore. This coincided with a boom in the Los Angeles population: between 1900 and 1920, the population increased from 170,000 to one million. Thus, the fishing industry expanded, and there was a new workforce prepared to take advantage of the opportunity to make a profit.[1]

The first World War would heighten demand for canned sardines and lead to a surge in catches topping 150,000,000 pounds by 1918. This is because the war would halt the North Sea sardine fishery. California fisheries stepped in, and produced sardine catches of 71,000 metric tons by 1918. As early as 1913, however, the reduction process in the canning industry was already being used for sardines at great profit.[2]

---

[1] Milton S. Love, "Subsistence, Commercial, and Recreational Fisheries" in *The Ecology of Marine Fishes: California and Adjacent Waters* (University of California Press, Berkeley, 2006): 567-594.

[2] Ibid.

Canning and reduction processes would revolutionize the California fishing industries for Pacific sardine and the tunas. The demand for canned sardines between 1913 and 1918 was significant, but reduced sardines were in even greater demand. Reduction involved converting waste parts to oil and fishmeal, and then canning the reduced sardines, which were sold as a food source. The sardine oil produced in the reduction process had a ready market in the paint and soap industry, and farmers used fishmeal as chicken feed. Thus, profits in canning reduced sardines surged, which meant that people who worked in the industry generated significant incomes.[3]

J.H. Blake developed an immediate enthusiasm for fishing that was infectious. He secured licenses to operate motorboats and began regularly taking the family out on the sea for boating and fishing trips at Hermosa and Redondo Beach. Charles A. Blake, emotionally lost at sea after losing his wife and son to the will of the Mount-Harris clan, reclaimed himself on the waters of the Pacific Ocean. Encouraged by his father, Charles applied for a boating and fishing license. Soon enough, he was operating a boat called "Cutter" and working as a fisherman off the Hermosa Beach docks.

As Hermosa, Redondo, and San Pedro were close knit communities, the Blake family soon became well-known and recognized. In January 1914, the Blakes moved from Hermosa to the neighboring Redondo Beach, with J.H. and Charles working as successful fishermen. The Blakes also spent time in San Pedro, where J.H picked up some additional work.[4]

---

[3] Ibid. See also Port of Los Angeles, "The Smell of Money: The Story of the Fishing and Canning Industry of the Los Angeles Harbor Area." March 21, 2024. Documentary, 32:05. https://www.youtube.com/watch?v=D_Fzv6T6YWk.

[4] *Redondo Reflex*, January 16, 1914: "Mr. and Mrs. Blake, their daughter [Hattie Blake-Croy] and husband [Harold Croy] and their small son [Theodore Blake] expect to leave today for San Pedro. Mr. Blake is a contractor who expects to obtain more work in that city."

Mr. and Mrs. H. B. Blake, of Paso Robles, were the guests this week of Mr. and Mrs. J. H. Blake, of Hermosa. Mr. J. H. Blake spent Wednesday in Redondo on a business trip and they expect to remove to that city this week if their plans are fulfilled.

Redondo Reflex, Jan. 1, 1914

Charles was out on the ocean daily, and thus developed skill and fluency with boat operations and even water rescues. In March 1914, he was in Redondo Beach, fixing up his lines and cleaning up his boat after a fishing trip when he witnessed a boy fall into the ocean from Wharf No. 1. Acting quickly, Charles grabbed the boy and pulled him out of the water to safety. As reported in the *Los Angeles Times*, "if it had not been for the quick action of Charles Blake, a local fisherman, who went to the rescue, he would have drowned."[5]

This would not be the first time Charles participated in ocean rescues. In December 1914, the Blake family departed aboard the "Cutter" at 10-o-clock in the morning for Rocky Point to get abalones. The boat party included the Blakes—Mr. J.H., Mrs. Ada, Charles, Theodore, and Hattie—as well as two girls, Ruth Smith (aged 14) and Evelyn Miller (age 12). The Smith and Miller families were also well-known in the Redondo area. Hattie Blake took part in the outing as a visitor from San Pedro. She had married Mr. Harold Croy (a fellow motorboat operator) in December 1913 and went by "Mrs. Harold Croy."[6]

---

[5] *Los Angeles Times*, "Falls Into Sea," March 18, 1914.

[6] See the Appendix for the full newspaper articles which recount this incident: *Los Angeles Times*, "Searchlights Scour Seas," Dec. 17, 1914 and *Redondo Reflex*, "Night of Terror on Raging Ocean," Dec. 18, 1914.

In the afternoon, a rough storm hit with strong winds, rain, and dangerous waves, which pushed the boat nearly 200 yards out from the Hermosa Beach pier. The storm conditions made it impossible for the Blakes to bring the boat into safety, and the party was left stranded and frightened from late Wednesday afternoon until six-o-clock Thursday morning. Anglers Charles Shaw and Joe Sweeney spotted the distressed party and initiated a rescue on that morning, successfully bringing all aboard the boat to safety. Prior to the rescue, search parties had gone out throughout the night to find the missing party but were unsuccessful.

During that long and treacherous night, Mrs. Blake reported that she prayed and prayed, and felt that they had all been saved by the grace of God. Charles Blake was quite shaken by the experience, but he acted to protect everyone on the boat. He ripped off the sail to use as a cover and shelter against the wind and rain. He also strived to weigh anchor and gather up the life preservers for his family members and the two girls. He stated that four of the life preservers were carried away by the wind and waves, and that the anchor lost its hold amidst the strong gale.

The Blakes and the girls, Ruth and Evelyn, were all brought safely to the home of Mr. and Mrs. Shaw. The young girls were brave during the entire ordeal, and well cared-for in the aftermath by Mrs. Ada Blake and Mrs. Shaw. Charles Blake had done his utmost to shelter the youngest girl, Evelyn Miller, during the storm, and was ever so grateful when she was rescued from the boat safely and not worse for the wear.

This experience would impact Charles a great deal, and he and his father would become better and more cautious fishermen because of it. This experience also led Charles to meet young Evelyn Miller. It would not be the last time they crossed paths.

The terrifying sea rescue on December 18, 1914 impressed upon both J.H. Blake and his son, Charles, the importance of understanding weather conditions and boat operations. Regrettably, in February 1915, Charles' boat "Cutter" was smashed against the rocks during another storm at Redondo Beach, near Wharf No. 1. The Blakes were well-prepared for this result, however, and most importantly, none were injured. In fact, J.H. and Charles no longer feared the Pacific and its storms. The men made a daily effort to conquer the ocean's tides and learn the best conditions for fishing. In no time at all, J.H. established himself as a skilled angler: by January of 1915, he was already making record catches of mackerel and surf perch.

FISHING CRAFT BEACHED DURING THE PAST WEEK

A number of rowboats and small fishing craft have gone to pieces on the beach or been badly damaged during the week.

The motor boat cutter, owned by Charles Blake, went down Tuesday afternoon, to the bottom of the sea, not very far out from wharf No. 1. It was in this boat that the family of J. H. Blake had such a thrilling ocean experience in December, when a party of seven people was lost on the sea during a night of wild storms. The happy outcome of the story is still fresh in the minds of The Reflex readers. Blake stated he estimated his loss at $150, should the boat not be recovered.

Above: Redondo Reflex, Feb. 5, 1915.
Right: Redondo Reflex, Jan. 12, 1915.

ANGLERS MAKING RECORD CATCHES

FINE MACKEREL RUN AFFORDS A1 SPORT TO FISHERMEN WHO CROWD PIERS

Joy unconfined and unrestrained has reigned on the piers for a number of days for mackerel fishing has gone by leaps and bounds up into near-top records for the number obtained by scores of anglers.

Among some recent good catches were those made by E. L. Curtis, J. A. Worthington, C. A. and J. H. Blake, "Scotty" Gordon, "Dad" Churchill and R. C. Fritz. The last named also hooked on Friday, above pier No. 3, two perch which weighed together six pounds. C. E. Beebe landed another surf perch weighing about two pounds. C. H. Cannon had the best luck ever with jack smelts, Friday.

Indeed, by 1915, the Blake family was truly settling into their life in Redondo Beach and pleased with their decision to relocate from the Midwest to the California coast. J.H. had moved on from wholesale meat packing and had proven himself to be a highly successful and well-regarded fisherman. Charles, too, had adjusted to life on the docks and quickly acquired the skillset and knowledge that leant well to a career in boating and fishing. Soon, J.H. and Charles were bringing in substantial income to support the entire family.

It was more money than Charles had ever made in Kansas City. He began to save up, tucking away a portion of his salary and keeping it in a locked box in his bedroom. He put a slip of paper inside the box. It was a running list of the total amount. At the top of the slip of paper, Charles wrote, "For Frank H. Blake."

REALLY, DON'T YOU KNOW, FISHERMEN SHOULD WORRY

"How's fishing?" "Why, pretty good, thank you. I caught seventeen fine halibut when out in the boat Saturday, so I can't complain," said J. H. Blake to a friend.

"Did you weigh any of the fish?" queried Angler Churchill. "No, but I think some weighed—"

"Well, let me tell you friend, that I'm 'it' in the halibut class," interrupted Churchill. "Out on wharf No. 2, I landed a ten-pound halibut today" (Sunday).

Silence for the space of a minute. Blake brightened up and, "Oh, well, there are just as big fish in the sea as were ever caught," quoth he. So now he's casting bait for a classy halibut to nibble at sooner or later.

Left: Redondo Reflex, Aug. 3, 1915
Right: Redondo Reflex, July 23, 1915

GOOD CATCHES ARE OF DAILY OCCURRENCE

Mackerel, more mackerel and larger mackerel are the portion of the wharf fishers this week, and very few anglers who will forsake their downy couches in the early morning hours go home empty handed. Halibut, flounders and bass give variety and those who go out a mile or two in the small craft of the fishermen some the heavy weights.

A party of young ladies from Pasadena, caught two fine strings Wednesday morning and, for fear their friends would be skeptical when the tale was told, posed before a kodak manipulated by one of the number and were snap-shotted, fish, poles, fishing togs and all. They had witnesses who can supply affidavits if required.

Large halibut, flounders, sea bass and mackerel weighing three to five pounds are brought in by the professional fishers in goodly numbers and they are as fat as butter, tender as sanddabs (almost).

Mrs. Ada Crow-Blake was enjoying life in California as well. She became friends with the neighbors, including the Shaws and the Millers, and thus kept good society. She was really pleased, however, when her family members from Iowa and South Dakota came for a visit in February of 1915. Her father, A.B. Crow, had travelled with her sister, Mary and her baby niece, Alice, to stay with the Blakes for several months. It was an absolute joy to spend time with them. Her father, Aquilla Belt Crow, was a Civil War veteran and member of the Grand Army of the Republic ("GAR"), a prominent veterans' organization comprised of Union soldiers. In 1915, at the age of 78, he remained highly involved in the GAR and began to partake in the Redondo Beach community as a booster.[7]

Mrs. Blake's sister, Mary Crow-Belange, and niece Alice (Mary's young daughter) stayed for a visit until the end of May and then returned home to South Dakota. Mrs. Blake was saddened by their departure but was soon distracted by other family news. Her own daughter, Mrs. Harold Croy, who was then living in San Francisco, sent a telegram complaining of illness. Mrs. Blake grew concerned and travelled north straight away to be with her.[8]

As it turned out, Mrs. Harold Croy's illness was the cause for celebration: she was expecting her first child. In October, the Pullman family of Redondo Beach arranged a surprise baby shower for her, hosting a dainty luncheon with little stork decorations arranged prettily on the table. Mrs. Blake was in attendance, of course, along with other female friends and neighbors. Baby Vivian May Croy would be born on November 28, 1915.[9]

The Blakes' time in Los Angeles, California had thus been quite novel and adventurous since their arrival in 1913. With the fishing industry booming, J.H. and Charles were able to obtain ample work.

---

[7] *Redondo Reflex*, February 2, 1915; *Los Angeles Times*, February 7, 1915; *Redondo Reflex*, "Guests from a Distance," March 2, 1915: Redondo Reflex, June 1, 1915. See "Grand Army of the Republic and Kindred Societies: A Guide to Resources in the General Collections of the Library of Congress" for information on the GAR (https://guides.loc.gov/grand-army-of-the-republic).

[8] *Redondo Reflex*, June 1, 1915; June 18, 1915; and October 19, 1915.

[9] State of California, California birth index entry for Vivian M. Crow in *California Birth Index, 1905-1995* (Sacramento, CA, USA: State of California Department of Health Services, Center for Health Statistics).

As nervous and broken as Charles had felt upon joining his family in Hermosa, his time out on the sea strengthened his resolve to be a good man and a good father. He did not have a wife any longer—Warren B. Harris had seen to that—but he still had a son and a duty to provide for that child. He felt that he could still provide for his son, even from a distance.

Around Christmastime 1915, Charles drafted a letter to Mr. Charles Mount of Kansas City, Missouri. It was brief. Charles stated that he and his family were in California and that he was making a good living as a fisherman. He then asked Mr. Mount to please accept an enclosed gift for Frank H. Blake, to be used for the boy's care and education. He did not mention Nona, nor did he ask to hear about the boy's wellbeing, or even for a response letter. Charles did not expect anything from the Mounts. It was enough that he was trying to do the right thing.

To Charles' great surprise, he would receive a note from Mr. Mount in early 1916. It merely said, "Thank you." From then on, Charles would send monthly contributions his son. At times, he thought about Nona Mount, the young girl who he had once loved. In his mind and heart, he was still married. Thus, although his neighbors in Redondo Beach tried to introduce him to their eligible young daughters, he rebuffed these invitations and focused on his work. He had no idea how much his life and circumstances would change in the coming months and years.

CHAPTER 8

1915
Kansas City, Missouri

While the fishing industry thrived in Los Angeles, California, the graphic arts industry thrived in Kansas City, Missouri. Graphic arts—to include commercial printing and associated trades of lithography, typesetting, engraving, photography, and filmmaking—became a highlight of the Kansas City business district in the early twentieth century. According to historical surveys of Kansas City, major players in the graphic arts industry were located between 6th and 14th Streets, bounded by Broadway to the west and Main to the east, for over six decades. These "major players" included printing and publishing companies such as the Standard Printing Company, Breeders Printing Company, and the Nelson-Hanne Printing Company. These companies fell under the umbrella of Kansas City's Graphic Arts Organization which represented approximately three thousand people employed in the industry. It provided "business counsel; legal, credit, and collection services; employment and organization matters; educational work; accounting, cost finding, and statistical activities; and cooperation in all matters related to the industry as a whole."[1]

The industry had such a strong presence by the 1910s that the Pratt-Thompson Investment Company decided to fund the construction of a brand new building that could serve as headquarters for the Graphic Arts Organization, and as the hub and incubator for all commercial printing enterprises. [2] Pratt-Thompson was a conglomerate comprising of an investment company as well as a construction company.

The city had a vested interest in funding the graphic arts—particularly newspapers and advertising—so Pratt-Thompson was prepared to contract with the best architects and planners they could procure.

---

[1] United States Department of the Interior: National Park Service, *National Register of Historic Places: Graphic Arts Building, Jackson County, Missouri.*

[2] Ibid.

City negotiations began in early 1915. By late February, contracts were signed, and construction was underway for what was proposed to be a seven-story Graphic Arts Building. According to the *Kansas City Star,* "the building [was] being erected by the Pratt-Thompson Construction Company. It has been sublet to printing houses and to firms in closely allied crafts." The site for construction was Tenth and Wyandotte.

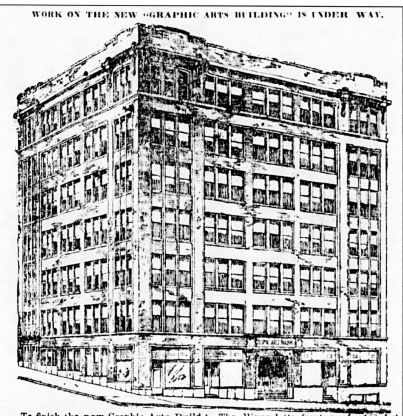

WORK ON THE NEW "GRAPHIC ARTS BUILDING" IS UNDER WAY.

To finish the new Graphic Arts Building at the northwest corner of Tenth and Wyandotte streets, by July 1, three shifts of workmen will be employed that the pouring of concrete may proceed without interruption.

The building is being erected by the Pratt-Thompson Construction Company. It has been sublet to printing houses and to firms in closely allied crafts. This has necessitated special construction in concrete, as various floors will be called upon to support 10-ton presses in action.

The Wyandotte frontage is 100 feet, the Tenth Street frontage 112 feet, with an extension, 28x40 feet, not disclosed in the picture. Each of the seven stories and the basement will have 9,500 square feet of floor space. The cost will be about $150,000.

A 2-story annex will be built to the west at this time and a still higher annex may be erected on an adjacent lot, buildings having been razed for the purpose, although the plans have not been definitely approved.

S. B. Tarbet is the architect.

Kansas City Star, March 7, 1915.

Correlia M. Thompson, wife of Edwin H.L. Thompson (President and General Manager of Pratt-Thompson), approved of the project and had a vested interest in its outcome. Mr. Thompson "gifted" the Graphic Arts Building to Correlia and gave her the authority to dictate its artistic design. Mr. Thompson had selected well-known city architect Samuel B. Tarbet to draw up the plans and serve as lead architect for the entire project. Tarbet submitted his plans to the Thompsons for approval, but ultimately designed the building for Correlia.[3]

The timeline for completion was July 1, 1915. This deadline was sufficient to construct the building as planned with seven stories. By May, Tarbet was on target for timely completion. The construction workers and engineers employed on the project were well-compensated. There were three shifts of workmen at the construction site daily, pouring concrete. Reports stated that the detached smokestack for the building, 135 feet in height, was poured in fourteen days. *Star* reporters commented that "building these giant stacks is something of an art and certain contractors specialize in them."[4] Other firms involved in the construction of the Graphic Arts Building included Hydraulic Press Brick Company based in St. Louis, manufacturers of the Hy-tex Brick; Automatic Sprinkler Company of America; Empire Electric Company; the Western Terra Cotta Company; and the Arkansas Bridge Company.[5]

---

[3] US Federal Census record for Edwin H.L. Thompson and Correlia Thompson, Kansas City, MO, 1910, listing Mr. Thompson's occupation as real estate and land. See also WWI draft registration card for E. H.L. Thompson, stating his employment as President & General Manager of Pratt-Thompson Construction Co. and listing Correlia M. Thompson as his wife. Edwin "Leo" Thompson married Correlia Mason in a society wedding in 1898. See Marriage Record for Correlia Mason and E.H. Leo Thompson, Jackson County Clerk, Kansas City, Missouri. See *National Register of Historic Places: Graphic Arts Building, Jackson County, Missouri*, stating that architect Tarbet designed the Graphic Arts Building for the owner, Correlia M. Thompson.

[4] *Kansas City Star*, "A Giant's Pipe Cast in Fourteen Days," May 19, 1915.

[5] National Register of Historic Places: Graphic Arts Building, Jackson County, Missouri.

As funder for the project, Pratt-Thompson had the power to alter the plans at a moment's notice. It did just that. As Tarbet was overseeing final construction, Pratt-Thompson decided that the building should have an additional eighth story. The eighth floor would be reserved for the Kansas City Graphic Arts Organization. Pratt-Thompson took out a building permit for this in August, thus pushing back the final completion date to December 31, 1915. The final story would be constructed of brick and concrete and add a cost of $5000. to the $150,000. project.[6]

Pratt-Thompson also had the power to hand-pick the contractors, including the third-party company solicited to install elevators within the building, Otis Elevator. Otis had been employed on various other projects in Kansas City, including elevator installation for Union Station. In operation since 1853, it quickly became the largest and most reputable national supplier of elevators.

Samuel B. Tarbet & Co.

ARCHITECTS

507-8 REPUBLIC BUILDING

Office Phone, Home 8117 Main   KANSAS CITY, MO.

Otis Elevator Company

MANUFACTURERS

PASSENGER, FREIGHT AND HAND POWER

ELEVATORS

Tels. Bell Grand 430-431, Home Main 1665   1918-20 Wyandotte Street

Listings in the 1915 Kansas City, MO city directory

---

[6] National Register of Historic Places: Graphic Arts Building, Jackson County, Missouri; *Kansas City Times*, "Graphic Arts Building to be 8 Stories," August 10, 1915.

Pratt-Thompson hired Otis as general contractor for the building's elevator system, consisting of a passenger elevator with a 2,500-pound capacity and two freight elevators with 5,000-pound capacity each. The building did not have a power plant, but steam heat was installed via a water tank in the basement. The type of elevator most likely used based on the technology available in the building was the hydraulic elevator.[7]

In the latter nineteenth century, Otis developed hydraulic elevators with rope-and-pulley systems, new braking technology, and steel guides. The electric elevator largely superseded hand-powered and steam-powered elevators by the twentieth century, however these types continued to be installed in buildings that lacked viable electric currents. Otis promoted hydraulic passenger and freight elevators propelled by water and steam as "designed to meet the requirements of high buildings, and on account of its economy in operation, very high speed, and the extreme rapidity with which stops and starts can be made, ranks high among hydraulic elevators." By the 1910s, the safety stopping device in the elevators had not materially changed from that which had been tested and installed thirty years earlier. Yet, Otis put great stock in their safety devices, employing safeguards against all known forms of elevator accidents.[8]

---

[7] Ibid.

[8] See Otis Elevator publication, *Otis Elevator Company : the Otis elevator industry comprises large manufacturing plants in the principal cities in the United States, Canada, Great Britain, Germany and France* 1903).

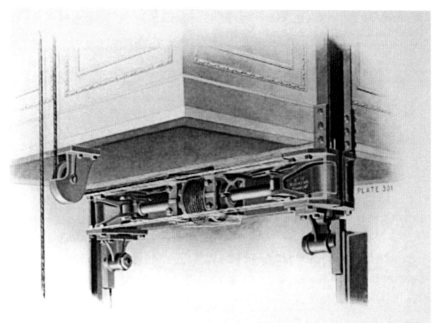

Fig. 23.   Safety Clutch for Steel Guide Posts.

Diagrams of the safety clutch. Otis Elevator's 1903 manual states the clutch is located at the top of the elevator hatchway and is suitably connected to the car, entirely independent of the lifting cables.

Fig. 24. Safety Clutch for Wooden Guide Posts.

Investment and construction companies that contracted with Otis Elevator (like Pratt-Thompson) relied on quality assurance and trust that the elevators would be installed with safety devices and controls that complied with reasonable standards of safety. The term "reasonable" applied in the lack of elevator industry codes and standards. National regulation of elevators did not exist until the American Society of Mechanical Engineers ("ASME") took the initiative to advance and promote standards of engineering.

ASME was established in 1880 and formed its first committee on performance test codes in 1884. It began to develop safety codes and standards for steam boilers, gas and oil engines, steam engines, and cranes. It was not until January 1921 that ASME issued its first safety code for elevators, the "A17." This code was not final: ASME submitted it to the American Engineering Standards Committee ("AESC") and subcommittees for revision and approval. The process was lengthy and involved multiple meetings and rounds of revision.[9] In July 1925, the AESC approved the final revised version of the elevator safety code ("A17-second edition"), which was published as the American standard for elevators then in production.[10]

Codes would change frequently with modernization over the years, but the 1925 A17 was the first national set of standards developed to "provide for the safety of life and limb, and to promote the public welfare." The code required compliance by elevator industry equipment manufacturers, installers, and maintainers. Noncompliance could result in statutorily imposed fines.[11]

In 1915, Otis Elevator was thus not bound by any safety codes, nor was Pratt-Thompson required to ensure that the elevator operators and maintainers it hired complied with safety regulations. This was the case despite ongoing reports of elevator accidents in Kansas City.

---

[9] Robert S. Caporale, "North American Elevator Industry Codes and Standards: A history on the governing standard in North America and explanation of how it is put together," *Elevator World* (March 2016); "Standards and Certification Chronology: Defining Events in ASME Standards & Certification" ASME Standards and Certification Chronology, accessed May 9, 2024, https://www.asme.org/codes-standards/about-standards/history-of-asme-standards/codes-and-standards-chronology. The A17 would be adopted by all government agencies (e.g., Dept. of Labor, Dept. of the Interior) as the federal standard for elevator safety.

[10] Ibid.

[11] Ibid.

How to Avoid Elevator Accidents.

To The Star: When the Rev. C. H. White was crushed to death Monday in that elevator accident, a beautiful life went out as one of the prices society must pay for its mania for speed. In order to make greater speed and thus please the public generally, the elevator boys close the doors on the run, after the cars have started. What cares the public for human life if its lust for speed can be gratified?

It should be a criminal offense to start an elevator until the door is closed and securely locked. This one defect in the elevator rules of Kansas City results in crushing someone every few months.

Kansas City Star, May 14, 1914. Comment submitted to the *Star,* critical of the lack of standards re: elevator operation, which has led to often fatal accidents.

Elevator installations in buildings throughout the country were commonplace during this time, however, and safety standards had not caught up with the pace of modernization. Companies like Pratt-Thompson moved forward on construction projects with zeal and ample funding, without concern for potential liability for accidents.

Amidst the fervor around the Graphic Arts Building, Nona Mount-Blake continued to reside at home with her parents and son while working in the printing industry. She had worked for a couple of printing and publishing firms since 1913, either as a cylinder feeder or a binder. The work was tolerable, though she did not have an opportunity to edit or otherwise move beyond clerical work. At the *Smithville Democrat-Herald,* W.B. Harris had allowed her to work as a compositor, assisting in preparing the paper for print. He had allowed Anna the same opportunity at the *Higginsville Jeffersonian.* And now, he was already bringing his young son, Howard, into the *D.H.* office and teaching him the trade (or so Anna had said in her letters).

Nona had developed an unease about her brother-in-law since that terrible time in 1913. Still, she could not argue with the fact that he was a superb businessman and employer, and a most devoted husband and father. And even though Nona had acted more reserved around him, he still inquired after her wellbeing, brought gifts for her son, Hurwitt, and showed the utmost respect for her father whenever he came into Kansas City, which was quite often.

He had stopped by the Mount residence in January 1915 from Higginsville, on his way back to Smithville. He was in rather high spirits, having just visited with Forrest and Edith Livesay and their two-year-old daughter, Leta. He had also stopped at Lee Shippey's home for dinner, where the two had spent the whole evening trading quips and finding humor in everything. "Uncle Bernie Harris of Smithville is struck by paradox that a spoiled child may be very fresh. And Uncle Bernie visited at our house recently too," Lee Shippey told the *Kansas City Times*.[12]

W.B. Harris passed through Kansas City again in April, and he was in a jovial mood when he joined Nona and her son, Hurwitt, at the kitchen table for the boy's afternoon treat. W.B. had brought Hurwitt a darling navy-blue coat with large metal buttons and a matching knitted hat. "Gifts from Annie," he explained. "To keep this young fellow warm against this Spring chill." Nona could not help but giggle as W.B. gently fitted the hat onto Hurwitt's head, and Hurwitt looked up at his uncle with big, inquisitive eyes and a small smile forming on his lips. She suspected, too, that the gifts were from W.B. himself. He enjoyed buying expensive gifts for everyone, but especially for the children. His own son, Howard, had a full wardrobe fit for a king. It warmed Nona to know that Howard, and Anna, were so loved and cared for.

"So, I've seen your sister, Belle," W.B. commented, turning his attention back to Nona. "Doing very well, though she misses you and Anna and Edna."

"Well, we shall have to arrange a visit soon. I'll send a note to Edna."

---

[12] *Kansas City Times*, January 5, 1915.

"Yes, I think that would be very good," W.B. agreed. "Perhaps you can pay a visit to Forrest and Edith as well. They are as happy as can be—Higginsville suits them—and as much as I hate to say it, Forrest fits in very well at the *Jeffersonian.* I had high hopes of bringing him back to the *D.H.*, but it seems that is not be." He paused for a few moments, looking thoughtful. "But perhaps I'll have better luck with someone else." His eyes gleamed as he looked at Nona.

She sensed the change in his expression and suddenly grasped what he was intimating. "Bernie—" she began.

"Nona, why the hell don't you come back and work at the *D.H.?*" W.B. interrupted. "You'll have a position there as compositor—just say the word." He looked oddly sad for a moment, which surprised Nona, and then his voice grew softer. "Annie would love it, you know. She feels that you've been so…" He paused again, trying to land on the right word. "…so independent. We understand that you want to make it on your own, and that you're comfortable here in Kansas City. But life could be so easy for you if—"

"Bernie," Nona murmured emphatically, and reached her hand to cover his. "I love the both of you dearly, but after what happened with…" She paused then, lowering her voice to a whisper. "After what happened with Charles, I just needed some time." Her expression grew sad and heavy for a moment, and she blinked to clear it. "And I've found myself since then. I have a good place here, with my parents and my boy. And I've been able to find good work. In fact…" She looked doubtfully at W.B., as if unsure if he accepted her answer; unsure if he wanted her to continue. But he looked at her with kindness, encouraging her to speak her mind.

"Well," she resumed, "I've been working for the Lechtman Printing Company. It's steady work, and I get good wages. My employer there, Mr. Campbell, likes my work. He plans to leave and go into business with another man in printing— Mr. Gates. They're going to start their own printing firm, Campbell-Gates."

W.B. nodded. "Yes, I've heard rumors. Mr. William Campbell and Mr. George Gates, you're referring to?"

"Yes," Nona replied. "Well, you see, Mr. Campbell has asked me to join them, to work for them. They're moving to the sixth floor of the new Graphic Arts Building." She said this last bit quickly, and looked at W.B., trying to gauge his reaction.

He was uncharacteristically quiet. This surprised Nona, so she asked, "Well, what do you think?"

W.B. looked at Nona with an odd expression in his eyes. There was love there, but also something else. Regret? Sadness? She could not tell.

He shifted in his seat at the table and folded his arms across his chest. "Campbell and Gates are fine businessmen. And to obtain a space in that new building is an accomplishment. But what I think has no bearing here. It's your choice, Nona. You must decide whether to take them up on their offer."

Nona was more shocked at his response than by anything he had ever said or done before. She was, in fact, a little hurt by his seeming indifference. "Bernie, you must have some opinions. Please—won't you tell me what I should do?"

W.B. lifted his gaze to consider her. She was pouting a little, her dark eyes large and pleading, as if she was a little girl who was disappointed when her favorite blanket was taken away.

He had his opinions, and he had been forceful and direct in expressing them over the years. He yearned to tell Nona in that moment that joining Campbell-Gates was not the best choice. He yearned to change her mind and bring her home with him to Smithville, where she could resume her duties at the *D.H.* He could easily persuade her of how happy she would be, living with them. He could remind her how she wanted Hurwitt and Howard to grow up together. He could tell her how much Anna would be glad of her company. And he could ensure that she and Hurwitt remained happy, safe, and well provided for. He had all the money and connections in the world to make that a certainty.

He could have said all of this in response to Nona's question, but something stopped him. Something in the way that Nona had said, *"After what happened with Charles, I just needed some time,"* stopped him. He had interfered in her life before, and that had only made things more difficult for her, not easier. What right did he have to impose his thoughts on her now? Did he, and Anna, and the rest of the family, really know what was best for her? And because of this, because he loved her, he chose his words carefully.

"Nonie," he said softly. "I've interfered in your life, and with your choices, quite enough. You are grown up, and you must decide what is right for you."

She did not like this answer, and he could tell. But he stood up, embraced her and Hurwitt, and then he said he had to be going.

"I must get back to Smithville. There's a press meeting in Maryville tomorrow, and Annie and Howard are travelling there with me. I'll give them your love, all right?"

Before Nona could process what W.B. had said, he was out the door and in his car, on his way back to Smithville. Back to the life that she could have shared with him, Annie, and Howard.

Nona Mount-Blake joined the Campbell-Gates Printing Company as a feeder and binder in their new office on the sixth floor of the Graphic Arts Building, 934 Wyandotte Street, Kansas City, Jackson County, Missouri. Despite her initial misgivings, she was thrilled to be working in the new building, with its modern architecture, beautifully designed offices, and state-of-the-art passenger elevators.

City directory listings for Kansas City, MO, 1915, listing William N. Campbell working for Campbell-Gates Company at 606 Graphic Arts Building and Nona Blake working as a feeder and residing on Troost Ave. George W. Gates partnered with William N. Campbell to form Campbell-Gates. The WWI draft registration card for Gates, date Sept. 12, 1918, lists him as manager of Campbell Gates Printing Co. Campbell previously worked for Lechtman Printing Co. at 414 W. 6th St. in Kansas City, MO, per city directory dated 1911.

All tenants of the Graphic Arts Building in 1915 were associated with printing. They included a number of printing companies, stationers, lithographers, engravers, typesetters, photographers and print supply houses.

Meanwhile, W.B. Harris, Anna, and Howard travelled to the town of Maryville, Missouri for a press meeting during the month of April. W.B. was a prominent guest and presenter at the meeting.

PRESS MEETING NOTES

Among the journalistic families in Maryville for press meeting is that of W. B. Harris of the Smithville Democrat-Herald. The family includes Mrs. Harris and their son Howard. Smithville is one of the live towns of central western Missouri.

The Maryville Daily Forum, April 23, 1915.

Weekly Democrat Forum, May 6, 1915.

> **W. B. Harris in the Smithville Democrat-Herald:** Maryville, the best town in Northwest Missouri, barring none, entertained the Northwest Missouri Press Association last Friday and Saturday. Maryville has 6,700 of the best Missouri people, has 12 miles of paving, a "white way" ornamental street lighting system, and last but not least a live Commercial Club that goes after things for the town and gets them.

From then on, W.B.'s presence on the newspaper circuit only grew. He was requested to attend frequent press meetings and conferences. His reputation as an expert in advertising won him the appointment of secretary for the St. Joseph Advertising Club in September of 1915. Shortly thereafter, the Nelson-Hanne Printing Company, based in St. Joseph, solicited him to become their advertising manager. The position came with influence and a hefty monetary incentive. W.B. was thus pleased to accept. This led to another opportunity: in November, W.B. was asked to teach the class in advertising in the educational department of the Y.M.C.A. W.B. accomplished all of this while still steering the *Smithville Democrat-Herald*.[13]

The year thus proceeded swiftly, with new prospects presented before both Nona Mount-Blake and Warren B. Harris. There was an odd current in the air, however. The year 1916 would bring change and heartbreak that neither the Mount, Harris, nor Blake families were prepared for.

---

[13] *St. Joseph News-Press Gazette*, "Favor for President," September 29, 1915 and November 3, 1915. Harris remained proprietor of the *Smithville Democrat-Herald* until 1918.

CHAPTER 9

1916
Kansas City, Missouri
Los Angeles, California

❖

The winds of change blew good fortune to the Blake family in Redondo Beach, California in early 1916. J.H. Blake had established a prominent position as a most successful fisherman, and everyone in the Los Angeles area knew it. He was rewarded for his talent handsomely, and soon the Blakes were among the most comfortably situated families in Los Angeles. As such, J.H. Blake had the ability to provide for his family's wants and needs. He also had the ability to live on the beach if he wanted. And he did want that for his family.

Thus, in December 1915, the Blakes had moved from 302 El Redondo to apartments at Oceano, 216 Strand. The highly desirable area of "The Strand" consisted of beachfront property that only the well-to-do of Redondo Beach could afford. Wharf No. 1 was a popular fishing spot. The Blakes often fished from Wharf No. 1 even before moving to the Strand.[1]

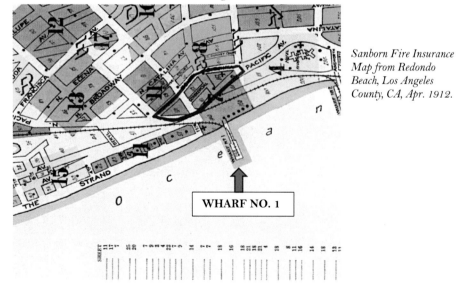

Sanborn Fire Insurance Map from Redondo Beach, Los Angeles County, CA, Apr. 1912.

WHARF NO. 1

---

[1] *Redondo Reflex*, January 7, 1916: "The J.H. Blake family moved last month from 302 El Redondo to apartments at the Oceano, 216 Strand"; "Saturday morning J.H. Blake, who now lives at 216 Strand, caught twenty-five perch and Sunday morning twenty-nine perch. He has also hooked yellowfin the past week."

> The most successful fisherman of all seems to be J. H. Blake whose luck is proverbial. In about three hours' time Thursday morning Blake hooked more than sixty perch that completely filled a large wash tub. It was a beautiful sight for the fish were uniformly large and their scales glistened like burnished gold and silver.
>
> Saturday afternoon more than a score of perch anglers had varying good fortune catching the beauties.

Redondo Reflex,
Jan. 18, 1916.

Charles A. Blake was likewise shaping up to be a skilled motorboat operator and fisherman, though did not claim to have the proverbial luck which his father seemed to possess. Still, his prowess with navigating the Pacific Ocean was irrefutable. Since he had lost his boat "Cutter" amidst the rocks and shoals in 1915, Charles had learned to study the weather conditions and anticipate an impending storm. He also calculated the best times to take his boat out for fishing and for leisure.

His parents and younger brother, Theodore, often accompanied him on boating trips. Soon enough, neighbors joined them as well. The girls Ruth Smith and Evelyn Miller—who had survived the raging storm in December 1914—joined them from time to time and did not exhibit the slightest fear. Young Evelyn liked to sit beside Charles as he steered the boat. He did not mind. She was a sweet young woman, and he enjoyed her company.

On an outing in March 1916, however, Charles was caught somewhat off guard by Evelyn. She had joined him and Theodore for some leisure fishing off the pier of Wharf No. 1. Charles was in the midst of teaching Evelyn how to hook a line when she looked up at him and asked, "Are you married?"

The question rattled him so much that he dropped the fishing line he was holding. "What makes you ask that?" he stuttered.

"Your sister is Mrs. Harold Croy—she took care of me and Ruth that night of the terrifying storm. I was wondering if there is a Mrs. Charles Blake. I would so like to meet her."

Evelyn's face was so earnest and innocent. As Charles looked back at her, his throat felt dry. His mind drifted to the last image he had stored of Nona Mount and his son, Frank.

He could not tell her the truth. He just couldn't. So, he just said, "No. No, I'm not." Evelyn just shrugged and turned her attention to Theodore, who had spotted a crab.

Later that evening, Charles composed a note to Mr. Charles Mount of Kansas City, Missouri, enclosing the usual monthly amount he sent for his son. He never asked about the boy's wellbeing, or about Nona. This time, though, he did.

He did not receive a response until about eight weeks later. It was a letter from Mr. Mount, and what it contained devastated him beyond comprehension.

The happenings in Kansas City and St. Joseph, Missouri in the spring of 1916 were rather different than those in Redondo, California. In March 1916, St. Joseph was gearing up for "Dress-Up Week," a nationwide event designed to promote public spending on new spring attire to boost the economy. As part of this effort, St. Joseph retail merchants resolved to declare March 31 through April 8, 1916 as the "spring dress-up…in cooperation with a similar campaign through the United States, promoted by the Dress-Up Bureau, Inc." The dress-up week movement would naturally lead to spending, but it would be advertised as a campaign for bettering dress and at the same time improving living conditions.

"Cleaner and better surroundings are conducive to better thoughts," the *St. Joseph Gazette* claimed, "and cleaner thoughts lead to cleaner living. All result in better health, more wholesome surroundings and progress along every practical line."[2]

The city of St. Joseph further promoted Dress-Up Week "with a view to encourage persons to purchase their spring apparel when stocks are the most complete and goods the freshest. It will be for the benefit of both the merchants and their patrons."[3]

As may be expected, a large event designed to increase spending during a one-week period required substantial and enticing advertising. St. Joseph needed a man who could oversee and manage advertisements that would encourage the public to buy. There was one man for the job who had a prominent presence in St. Joseph, and who had established himself as an expert in advertising.

That man was Warren B. Harris.

---

[2] *St. Joseph News Press*, "For a Dress-Up Week," March 6, 1916; *St. Joseph Gazette*, " 'Dress Up' Move is Sweeping Country," March 8, 1916.

[3] *St. Joseph News Press*, "For a Dress-Up Week," March 6, 1916.

W.B. had been appointed advertising manager for the Nelson-Hanne Printing Company in 1915 and had since established substantial credibility. In March 1916, he was appointed chairman of the advertising committee for Dress-Up Week, tasked with publicity features and formulating plans to "properly exploit the event."[4] He spent weeks in St. Joseph fulfilling this role, as well as carrying on with his duties for Nelson-Hanne.

In the third week of April 1916, he returned home to Smithville with large bags filled with hats, gloves, scarves, a new gown for Anna, and a complete business outfit for Howard (pants, shirt, vest, shoes, and top hat). When Anna met him at the door, looking astonished and chastising him for spending so much money, he only smiled and said, "I spent a little, and it was all for the public good."

Anna shook her head, but nonetheless began pulling the clothes out of the bags, her eyes lighting up in delight as she did so. She adored dressing up and displaying the latest fashions, and W.B. knew it. "We should give some of this to Nonie when we visit in a couple weeks," she exclaimed, as she selected a hat and a pair of gloves that she felt would suit her sister perfectly. "Lord knows I have too many hats."

"That may be true," W.B. chuckled. "But you do wear them so well." He selected a rather stylish pine-green velvet hat adorned with a feather from the pile of clothing and placed it on her head.

Anna smiled. "And you spoil me—Howard and me both."

"Of course I do, and why shouldn't I?" he admitted, kissing her lightly on the cheek. "Now, I must fetch our son," he continued, grinning more broadly. "It's off to the office we go."

Anna laughed, shaking her head. "Soon he'll be running circles around you at that paper of yours."

"That *is* the plan, my dear," he replied.

---

[4] *St. Joseph Gazette*, "Women to Assist in Dress Up Week; Need Strong Publicity," March 15, 1916.

W.B. was a fine mentor to Howard and delighted in showing him around the *D.H.* office. He had plans to show him around the *Jeffersonian* and the *Star* as well.

And so he would—the Harrises would visit Higginsville and Kansas City for several weeks in May. It was a visit they greatly looked forward to, providing them an opportunity to spend time with friends and family. Anna especially was glad of the time she would spend with Nona and her son, Hurwitt. It had been too long since they had been together as sisters, and longer still since Hurwitt and Howard had played together.

At the time of planning this visit, W.B. and Anna were unaware just how important it would be to spend that time with Nona Mount.

Since their arrival in Kansas City in the first week of May, the Harrises spent ample time with the Mount family, as well as with the Sauvains.

Guy P. Sauvain was employed in shoe sales and repairs at Royal Shoe Shop at 605 E. 31st Street. He was devoted to his craft and remained as charming, handsome, and witty as ever. Anna Harris learned that he had also, in recent months, visited with the Mounts and taken a shine to young Frank Hurwitt Blake. His warm nature and attentiveness made him a popular and most welcome visitor—even Mr. Charles Mount enjoyed Guy's company.

In that Spring of 1916, Guy Sauvain remained unmarried, though tended to inquire about Edna Mount-Stamm whenever he visited with the Mounts. In time, Guy would be unabashedly pleased to hear that Edna and Frank Stamm had separated. Guy and Edna would meet again a short time after, and their compatibility could not be denied.

Nona Mount-Blake, meanwhile, remained an independent working woman. She had begun employment at Campbell-Gates in the Graphic Arts Building in the early fall of 1915. Her employers, William Campbell and George Gates, ran a busy printing office and Nona worked long hours at the printing press.

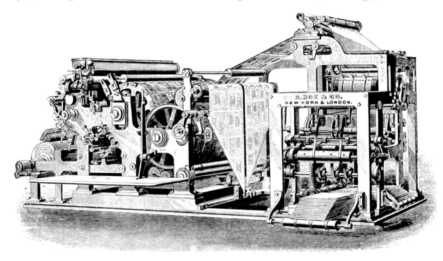

NEWSPAPER AND PAMPHLET PRESS

Source: Robert Hoe, A short history of the printing press: and of the improvements in printing machinery from the time of Gutenberg up to the present day (New York, 1902): 81.

While Nona was at work, she left her son, Frank Hurwitt Blake, in her parents' care. Charles and Samantha Mount loved the boy and provided him with anything he may need, including their undivided attention. Between this, the regular visits from Guy Sauvain, and the frequent gifts from W.B. Harris, little Frank Hurwitt was always surrounded by people who adored him.

When the Harrises came into Kansas City to stay with the Mounts, Anna gladly looked after both Hurwitt and Howard. The boys were around the same age— Hurwitt was nearly four, and Howard was five—and played well together.

On the morning of May 16, 1916, Anna had planned a fun outing for them. She would take the boys to lunch in town and then they would spend the afternoon in the park. Afterwards, they would come home to have dinner as a family, just in time for Nona to come home after work. W.B. Harris was busy, out and about town, going to the *Star* offices for meetings and placing calls to Smithville to ensure his employees were on track to publish the weekly issues of the *D.H.* In the morning, he usually sat at the Mounts' kitchen table, sipping coffee, and reading the morning issue of the *Star.*

On the morning of May 16, 1916, W.B. was following this routine per usual, and waiting for Anna and Nona to greet him. They were both busy that day, however, and barely had a moment to wish him good morning. Anna was dressing the boys, and Nona hurried out of the house in a rush without so much as glancing at W.B.

Nona hastened down the street to catch a jitney to the Graphic Arts Building, her boots clicking on the pavement. She was dressed in a new outfit that Annie and W.B. had gifted to her: a long charcoal grey skirt with buttons sewn neatly at the waist and a white blouse, as well as a matching grey hat and grey stockings. Nona had said that the gift was too much, but W.B. insisted that she accept it. Everything had been purchased on sale in St. Joseph during dress-up week, Annie assured her. The quality of the clothing was so fine that Nona was sure W.B. had nonetheless spent a fortune on it, and on the items he had brought for Hurwitt. Nona was proud to look so put together, and she carried herself confidently as she descended from the jitney and approached the building.

She had been prepared to ascend to the sixth floor as usual, feeling attractive and confident, but then something in the air shifted. She could only describe it as a feeling of misgiving, and she remembered seeing a boy hovering in the shadows near the elevator.

The remainder of the day proceeded as usual, and she was occupied with various tasks around the Campbell-Gates office. She worked efficiently and planned to depart at a quarter to five-o-clock. She had been working in the building for eight months, and she knew the schedules of the doormen and the elevator operators. If she boarded the elevator at a quarter to five, as she always did, then the daytime elevator operator would be on duty. There was a shift change that happened between 4:55 p.m. and five-o-clock. Nona did not know who operated the elevators after five-o-clock. She had never been at the office that late, except for on the evening of May 16, 1916.

Something began to go wrong as the day drew to a close. Anna Harris had placed a call to Campbell-Gates at 4:40 p.m., asking to speak to her sister, Nona. A man in the office had answered and refused the request, stating that Mrs. Blake would be clocking out for the day soon. Nona was never given the message that her sister had called. As she was walking out the door with her belongings at a quarter to five, Mr. Campbell detained her. He spoke to her for a good seven minutes. Nona was anxious to leave and arrive home on time, but Mr. Campbell was her employer. She had to wait until he released her.

By the time Nona reached the elevator, it was 4:55 p.m. There was no one on duty to operate the elevators, as far as Nona knew. But then a young man appeared, someone she did not recognize. He did not announce his name and he claimed that he was a new elevator operator on staff. In her anxiousness to arrive home, Nona boarded the elevator with him.

The young man was named Benjamin F. Grove. He was employed as a janitor for the Graphic Arts Building. The daytime elevator operator had left for the day at 4:50 p.m. There was no one scheduled to replace him for the rest of the evening, and yet many tenants remained in the building who would need to take the elevator to the first floor. Grove filled in to operate the lift that evening, despite having no training or experience.

There was a boy, about nine years old, in the elevator when Nona stepped in. His name was Boyd Fulton, and he was an office boy for the John Reed Printing Company located on the sixth floor of the Graphic Arts Building. There was no reason why the boy was in the elevator. He was young and should have gone home for the day already. He was not even noticed by Grove until it was too late. But he was just a little boy. He did not know how it happened and had no ability to stop it.

U.S., City Directories, 1822-1995 for Benjamin F Grove
Missouri › Kansas City › 1916 › Kansas City, Missouri, City Directory, 1916

Grove Agnes teacher Greenwood School r 4205
Windsor av
Grove A M lab Park Board r 222 Gillis
Grove Benjamin F janitor Graphic Arts Bldg

BELL MAIN

KODA

U.S., City Directories, 1822-1995 for Boyd Fulton
Missouri › Kansas City › 1915 › Kansas City, Missouri, City Directory, 1915

Fulton Blanche bkpr r Roxford Hotel
Fulton Boyd printer John W Reed r 805 Forest
Fulton Bros (Charles W and Richard T) real
estate 1114 Clard Bldg

The elevator malfunctioned. It was meant to descend from the sixth floor to the first floor. Instead, it ascended a foot above the seventh floor and then stopped on "safety," meaning that the safety clutch became stuck. Grove had to go to the loft to release the clutch and the car from "safety." Grove had no experience in operating the switches that controlled the cars. He left the controller in the elevator on "neutral," believing that this would keep the car stationary while he released the clutch. The car should have been held in place until Grove returned and taken the controller out of "neutral."

Something happened when Grove was in the loft, trying desperately to sort out the switches and what they controlled. He vacillated for a few moments and then just pushed one switch in place. That did not seem to accomplish anything, so he removed the switch altogether, believing that this would release the car from "safety."

Grove realized his mistake almost immediately. With his heart hammering and the adrenaline pumping in his veins, he did the only thing he could think of to stop the now-moving car. He broke the circuit and threw off the power entirely. These actions caused the car to lurch forward, and then plummet downwards from the seventh floor to the sixth floor.

Grove heard the cries and the screaming even before he reached the seventh floor. The sight he encountered shocked him. The car had halted to a grinding stop on the sixth floor when Grove threw off the power. The woman, Mrs. Nona Mount-Blake, was lying with her body somehow ensnared at the top of the cage. It was only then, as Grove was staring in horror and disbelief at Mrs. Blake, that he noticed the office boy, Boyd Fulton.

Fulton thought Mrs. Blake was a nice and pretty woman, and he was only trying to help. He did not know she would fall forward like that. He remembered that she had placed her hands in front of her to stop herself from falling just as the car lurched forward and began to plummet downwards. He had been thrown to the back of the car as soon as it moved. But Mrs. Blake had been standing near the cage door. The moment the car lurched, Fulton called out to Mrs. Blake to step backwards, and he tried to reach for her. But something went wrong. The car was moving too quickly, and the lights in the car went out when the power was thrown. Mrs. Blake began to fall before he realized what has happening.

The last thing Nona felt was sheer panic as she held her hands forward to stop herself from falling forward. And the last thing she thought about was her family waiting up for her at home, and the faded memory of Anna catching her when she was a child.

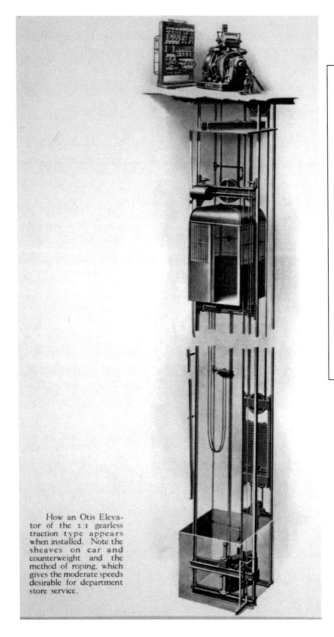

How an Otis Elevator of the 2:1 gearless traction type appears when installed. Note the sheaves on car and counterweight and the method of roping, which gives the moderate speeds desirable for department store service.

Otis Elevator publication: Moving your customers and what they buy. brief suggestions for increasing business by improving service. (1915), p. 6-7.

"How an Otis Elevator of the 2:1 gearless traction type appears when installed. Note the sheaves on car and counterweight and the method of roping, which gives the moderate speeds desirable for department store service."

Gearless traction hydraulic elevators were also used in office buildings.

The Mounts were living at 1420 Virginia Street in Kansas City in 1916. On the evening of May 16, 1916, Charles and Samantha Mount were at home, along with Anna Harris and the two boys, Hurwitt and Howard. W.B. Harris had not yet returned.

At about ten minutes after five-o-clock, as the family was preparing dinner and waiting for Nona and W.B. to arrive, there was a knock at the door. Charles Mount answered it. It was someone from Emergency Hospital, notifying him that his daughter, Mrs. Nona Blake, had been taken there in an ambulance and had sustained severe injuries in what appeared to be an elevator accident.

Dr. James I. Tyree, a local physician, saw Mrs. Nona Blake while in the ambulance on the way to Emergency Hospital. A man named Grove had called for the ambulance immediately and had helped to gingerly place Mrs. Blake inside. Dr. Tyree remembered that Grove had been shaken and his face was white. There was also a little boy standing behind Grove and crying hysterically. Dr. Tyree knew that the woman, Mrs. Blake, had not survived, but could not ascertain the exact cause of death.

The hospital emergency staff examined Mrs. Blake and there was nothing they could do to revive her or repair the damage. The extent of the injuries was far too great.

Mrs. Nona Mount-Blake was declared deceased at 5:03 p.m. on May 16, 1916. Her body had been crushed. The only saving grace, if any at all, was that she had been killed instantly and thus spared from the pain of the impact. That is what the attending doctor told Mr. and Mrs. Mount and Mr. Harris.

The grief and pain of the Mounts could be felt throughout the entire city. W.B. Harris was sickened and devastated beyond comprehension. All of the strength nearly went out of him as he stood by Mr. and Mrs. Mount. But he held onto his wits because he had to. He had to stay strong for the Mounts, and for Anna, and mostly, for Nona. She would not have wanted him to crumble underneath the waves of grief he felt. She would have wanted to know that her son was safe and spared from the reality of what had happened.

So, W.B. used the phone at the hospital to call Mrs. Edna Mount-Stamm and ask her if she could take both Hurwitt and Howard to stay with her for a while. She was the most level-headed of the Mount sisters in Kansas City and would see to it that the boys were safe and sheltered. She said yes, that it was no trouble at all, and that she would go to the house on Virginia Street immediately. When she asked W.B. what was wrong, his voice faltered, and he felt his throat contract. He had to tell her. He was scared to tell Annie, but he could tell Edna. She would know how to keep her composure and how to tell Annie, even if the news broke her heart into a thousand pieces. Edna Mount had the incredible ability to remain stoic amidst adversity—it was a quality she had inherited from her grandmother, Jane Mount.

Edna was of the same mind as W.B. She had to remain strong for the family, especially for Annie and the boys. Though she was still legally married to Frank Stamm at the time, the two had separated some months back. He no longer resided with her, and the divorce was well under way. Before leaving for the Mount residence, Edna placed a call to Guy Sauvain and asked him to meet her at the house. The call lasted no more than twenty seconds. Guy agreed to come immediately, no questions asked.

Edna would be the one to tell Anna Harris the news. Before she did, Guy took Hurwitt and Howard to sit outside on the porch so that they would not hear Anna's sobs.

It shook Anna to the core, and she was inconsolable. Edna would stay at the house on Virginia with Anna, W.B., and her parents for two weeks. During that time, Guy Sauvain drove Frank H. Blake and Howard B. Harris to the home of Richard M. Sebastian and Belle-Mount Sebastian in Higginsville. The Sebastians welcomed them with open arms and wholeheartedly assured Guy that they would care for the boys as long as was needed. Belle was even more stoic than Edna, and asked Guy how the family was holding up. She cared completely about their wellbeing, never mind her own.

The visit was brief, and Guy politely refused to stay overnight. He insisted on driving back to Kansas City so that he could support the Mount family, and to do whatever Edna needed him for. At that moment, Belle realized that Guy Sauvain loved her sister.

W.B. was away from the house during that week of May 16. The first order of business, in his mind, was to control the papers and ensure the news was publicized in the most respectful and accurate manner possible. There was no way to stop the reporters. They would all spin a version of what happened. They would all demand interviews from the people involved: the manager of the Graphic Arts Building, Nona's employer, the man who was operating the elevator, the boy who witnessed the accident, the attending doctor. This was going to happen, and there was no way to stop it. W.B. just needed to control the narrative.

He immediately went to Bill Nelson's office at the *Kansas City Star*. Nelson always worked late. He was not surprised when Harris knocked on his door at nine-o-clock on the evening of May 16. Nelson's own reporters had already gotten wind of the story and somehow obtained an interview of John H. Thompson, Jr., the manager of the Graphic Arts Building, and of William N. Campbell, proprietor of the Campbell-Gates Printing Company. Nelson shared a draft of the story he planned to publish in the *Kansas City Times*. He and Harris edited the story together. Their version was published in the May 17, 1916 issue.

W.B. strove to control the narrative, but there was only so much he could do in a short window of time. The *Kansas City Journal*, the *Kansas City Post*, and the *St. Joseph News Press Gazette* published their own stories on May 17, 1916. W.B. did not have time to place a call to his colleagues in St. Joseph before the story went out to print.

On May 17, after being up the entire night before, W.B. drove to Smithville. He went straight to his office at the *Smithville Democrat-Herald* and did not stop at home. He instructed his staff to prepare a publication that would go out on May 19. He then locked himself in his office and penned an obituary for his sister-in-law, Mrs. Nona Mount-Blake. The story appeared in the May 19, 1916 issue of the *Smithville Democrat-Herald*. It was very similar to the version the *Star* had published on May 17. The *Star* called W.B. late in the evening on the 17th to inform him that they had come upon more details and had enough to publish a follow-up story in the next morning's edition. An editor dictated the draft to W.B., and he approved it.

Death certificate for Mrs. Nona Mount-Blake:
Reports that Nona Blake was married and working in printing and book bindery. Date and time of death reported as May 16, 1916, 5:03 p.m. Cause of death reported as "crushed in elevator accident." Charles Mount, of 1420 Virginia St., signed off on the death certificate.

In order of publication: newspaper articles detailing the elevator accident:

ELEVATOR KILLED A WOMAN.

Mystery in Accident to Mrs. Nona Blake in Graphic Arts Building.

Mrs. Nona Blake, 24 years old, was fatally injured by an elevator on the sixth floor of the Graphic Arts Building, Tenth and Wyandotte streets, late yesterday. Her neck was dislocated and body crushed. She died thirty minutes later at the Emergency Hospital.

How Mrs. Blake met her death perhaps never will be known. None saw the accident. The cage passed the safety trip on the sixth floor and was held. The operator—known as "Red," whose other name was not known even to John H. Thompson, jr., manager of the building—had gone to the seventh floor to release the cage. It was lowered about three feet, according to Mr. Thompson. He said that it seemed Mrs. Blake had opened the shaft door that she might see what had caused the cage to stop. It was when the cage was lowered that the accident happened.

The version of the accident told by William N. Campbell of the Campbell-Gates Printing Company, who employed the young woman, differed from that of the building manager. He declared that Mrs. Blake must have been leaving the elevator when the accident happened. That fact, he said, was evinced by blood at the top of the steel door entering the shaft.

The elevator operator formerly was a fireman at the building, it was stated. He was working "extra" on the elevators.

Mrs. Blake was a widow. She lived with her parents, Mr. and Mrs. Charles Mount, 1420 Virginia Street. Besides her parents, she is survived by a son, Herbert, 3 years old, a brother, William Mount, 1243 Penn Street, and six sisters, one of them Mrs. Edward Stamm, 1420 Virginia Street.

Kansas City Times, May 17, 1916

WOMAN'S NECK BROKEN

Mrs. Nona Blake, Bindery Worker, Killed in an Elevator.

Mrs. Nona Blake, a bindery worker, was instantly killed at 5:30 o'clock yesterday afternoon in the passenger elevator of the Graphic Arts building, Tenth and Wyandotte streets. Mrs. Blake boarded the elevator on the first floor. It is believed the elevator started upward before Mrs. Blake was in it. Her neck was broken.

Dr. James Tyree of the emergency hospital, who arrived a few minutes after the accident, was unable to ascertain the exact cause of death.

Mrs. Blake was 23 years old and was employed by a book bindery firm in the Graphic Arts building. She lived at 1420 Virginia with a 3-year-old daughter. Her father is Charles Mount.

Kansas City Journal, May 17, 1916. Time of death is inaccurate; inaccurately states that Mrs. Blake had a three-year-old daughter.

WOMAN KILLED BY MOVING ELEVATOR

Attempts to Board It and Head Is Crushed Against Door.

Mrs. Nona Blake, 24 years old, was killed in an elevator accident at the Graphic Arts building late yesterday afternoon, apparently while she was attempting to board the moving lift. Benjamin F. Grove, elevator operator, made a statement to the police this morning. He was not held.

Grove said Mrs. Blake boarded the car at the sixth floor and rode up to the seventh. He said he stopped the car about a foot above the seventh floor and that it stuck there.

"I had to go up to the eighth floor and release the automatic brake and adjust the down feed," Grove said. "First, I helped Mrs. Blake off the car and left her standing three feet away. I left the elevator door open about six inches so I could get back, as it automatically locks when closed tight.

"When I started the down feed, the car started down, but did not stop at the seventh floor. I threw in the brake and it stopped. Then I heard someone scream.

"I found the car stopped midway between the sixth and seventh floors and Mrs. Blake was lying on top of the car with part of her body on the seventh floor."

Mrs. Blake's neck was broken and her head crushed. As the car started down it is believed she opened the door and attempted to get aboard and the moving car caught her head at the top of the door.

Grove said a boy was in the car when he ran down and the boy stood on the stool and opened the gate for him. He did not know the boy, or how he got in the car. Grove said he and the boy took Mrs. Blake off the top of the car and he held her until the ambulance came.

Mrs. Blake was a widow and lived with her parents, Mr. and Mrs. Charles Mont, 1420 Virginia avenue. A son, Herbert, 3 years old, a brother and six sisters also survive her.

Kansas City Post, May 17, 1916. Inaccuracies as to the name of Nona's parents (Mont instead of Mount) and the name of her son (Herbert instead of Hurwitt).

WOMAN KILLED BY ELEVATOR.

Employe of Kansas City Printing Company Is Decapitated When She Thrusts Head In Shaft.

KANSAS CITY, May 17.—Mrs. Nona Blake, twenty-nine years old, an employe of a printing company, was killed here last night in an elevator accident in a downtown building. It is believed she had put her head in the open door of the shaft to see what was wrong with the cage, which had been wedged at a floor above.

St. Joseph News Press Gazette, May, 17, 1916. Note the sensationalized language. This story was published quickly without ascertaining accurate information about what had occurred, and without running the story by W.B. Harris.

DEATH ELEVATOR IN MOTION.

Office Boy Was in Cage When Mrs. Blake Was Killed.

The details of the death of Mrs. Nona Blake in an elevator in the Graphic Arts Building, Tuesday afternoon, as told by Benjamin F. Grove, who was acting as elevator operator, and Boyd Fulton, vary only slightly.

Boyd Fulton, an office boy for the John A. Reed Printing Company, was the only witness to Mrs. Blake's death. Grove said he had picked Mrs. Blake up on his up trip at the sixth floor. When the car passed a foot above the seventh floor, it stopped on "safety," and it was necessary for him to go to the loft to release it.

He helped Mrs. Blake from the elevator, leaving the door nearly closed. He had left the controller on "neutral."

In the loft he pushed a switch in place and then removed it, to release the car from "safety." When the car did not stop, he broke the circuit and threw off the power, then ran down the steps to the seventh floor and found the car gone. He ran to the floor below.

The office boy, Boyd Fulton, whom he had not seen when he left the car, was on the inside of the stopped elevator. Grove, with assistance, took Mrs. Blake from the top of the cage. Young Fulton climbed from the car. He was near hysteria and was taken home.

Boyd Fulton explained his presence in the elevator. The door was open, he said, and Mrs. Blake was in the car. He entered and shortly after it started down, without the operator. Mrs. Blake, he said, leaped toward the door and grasped the beam supporting the door of the shaft. Her head was struck by the cage and her body turned to the top of the car. He had not touched the controller and had not seen Mrs. Blake touch it.

The body of Mrs. Blake will be taken today to Higginsville, Mo., for burial.

Kansas City Times,
May 18, 1916.

Fatal Accident

Mrs. Nona Blake, 24 years old, sister of Mrs. W. B. Harris of Smithville, was fatally injured by an elevator on the sixth floor of the Graphic Arts Building, Tenth and Wyandotte streets, Kansas City, Tuesday evening. Her neck was dislocated and body crushed. She died thirty minutes later at the Emergency Hospital.

How Mrs. Blake met her death perhaps will never be known. None saw the accident. The cage passed the safety trip on the sixth floor and was held. The operator—known as "Red," whose other name was not known even to John H. Tompson, jr., manager of the building—had gone to the seventh floor to release the cage It was lowered about three feet, according to Mr. Thompson. He said that it seemed Mrs. Blake had opened the shaft door that she might see what had caused the cage to stop. It was when the cage was opened that the accident happened.

The version of the accident told by William N. Campbell of the Campbell-Gates Printing Company who employed the young woman, differed from the building manager. He declared that Mrs. Blake must have been leaving the elevator when the accident happened. That fact, he said, was evinced by blood at the top of the steel door entering the shaft.

Mrs. Blake was a widow. She lived with her parents, Mr. and Mrs. Charles Mount, 1420 Virginia Street. Besides her parents, she is survived by a 3-year-old son, one brother and six sisters. Mrs. Blake worked on the Democrat-Herald for a short time.

Funeral services and burial at Higginsville, Mo., Friday morning, May 19th.

Smithville Democrat-Herald, May 19, 1916. This is W.B. Harris' account. Note the accurate details and the respectful tone of the story. Also note that Harris held fast to the narrative that Nona was a widow. Harris would have been aware of, and attended, the funeral services and burial for Nona.

LLE, LAFAYETTE COUNTY,

KILLED IN ELEVATOR ACCIDENT

Mrs. Nona Mount-Blake Met Almost Instant Death in Accident—Body Brought Here for Burial

The body of Mrs. Nona Mount-Blake who met death in an elevator accident at Kansas City Tuesday evening, was brought to Higginsville Thursday morning and taken to the home of her sister, Mrs. R. M. Sebastian on Fair Ground avenue. Funeral service will be held at the Second Baptist church Friday morning at 10:30 o'clock, conducted by Rev. A. J. Smith. Burial will be made in the city cemetery.

Deceased formerly lived here with her parents, Mr. and Mrs. Charles Mount. She was a sister to Mrs. R. M. Sebastian and Mrs. Fred Newman of this place, and there are also four other sisters, namely, Mrs. Fred Morgan and Mrs. Joe Jones of Corder; Mrs. Edward Stamm, Kansas City; Mrs. W. B. Harris, Smithville, Mo., and one brother, Wm. Mount, Kansas City, who survive her. The Kansas City Star Wednesday morning contained the following account of the accident:

Mrs. Nona Blake, 24 years old, was fatally injured by an elevator on the sixth floor of the Graphic Arts Building, Tenth and Wyandotte streets, late yesterday. Her neck was dislocated and body crushed. She died thirty minutes later at the Emergency Hospital.

How Mrs. Blake met her death perhaps never will be known. None saw the accident. The cage passed the safety trip on the sixth floor and was held. The operator—known as "Red," whose other name was not known even to John H. Thompson, Jr., manager of the building—had gone to the seventh floor to release the cage. It was lowered about three feet, according to Mr. Thompson. He said that it seemed Mrs. Blake had opened the shaft door that she might see what had caused the cage to stop. It was when the cage was lowered that the accident happened.

The version of the accident told by William N. Campbell of the Campbell-Gates Printing Company, who employed the young woman, differed from that of the building manager. He declared that Mrs. Blake must have been leaving the elevator when the accident happened. That fact, he said, was evinced by blood at the top of the steel door entering the shaft.

The elevator operator formerly was a fireman at the building, it was stated. He was working "extra" on the elevators.

Mrs. Blake was a widow. She lived with her parents, Mr. and Mrs. Chas. Mount, 1420, Virginia Street. Besides her parents, she is survived by a son, Herbert; 3 years old, a brother, William Mount, 1243 Penn street, and six sisters, one of them Mrs. Edward Stamm, 1420 Virginia Street.

Higginsville Advance, May 19, 1916:
"The body of Mrs. Nona Mount-Blake who met death in an elevator accident at Kansas City Tuesday evening was brought to Higginsville Thursday morning and taken to the house of her sister, Mrs. R.M. Sebastian on Fair Ground Avenue. Funeral service will be held at the Second Baptist Church Friday morning at 10:30 o'clock, conducted by Rev. A.J. Smith. Burial will be made in the city cemetery. Deceased formerly lived here with her parents, Mr. and Mrs. Charles Mount. She was a sister to Mrs. R.M. Sebastian and Mrs. Fred Newman of this place, and there are also four other sisters, namely, Mrs. Fred Morgan and Mrs. Joe Jones of Corder; Mrs. Edward [Frank] Stamm, Kansas City; Mrs. W.B. Harris, Smithville, MO; and one brother, [William] Mount, Kansas City, who survive her…" The rest of the article quotes the Kansas City Star.

VOL. 21   NO. 9

NONA MOUNT KILLED

Former Higginsville Girl in Kansas City Accident

Mrs. Nona Blake, 24 years old, was fatally injured by an elevator on the sixth floor of the Graphic Arts Building, Tenth and Wyandotte streets, Kansas City, Tuesday. Her neck was dislocated and body crushed. She died thirty minutes later at the Emergency hospital.

How Mrs. Blake met her death perhaps never will be known. None saw the accident. The cage passed the safety trip on the sixth floor and was held. The operator — known as "Red," whose other name was not known even to John H. Thompson, jr., manager of the building —had gone to the seventh floor to release the cage. It was lowered about three-feet, according to Mr. Thompson. He said that it seemed Mrs. Blake had opened the shaft door that she might see what had caused the cage to stop. It was when the cage was lowered that the accident happened.

The version of the accident told by William N. Campbell of the Campbell-Gates Printing Company, who employed the young woman, differed from that of the building manager. He declared that Mrs. Blake must have been leaving the elevator when the accident happened. That fact, he said, was evidenced by blood at the top of the steel door entering the shaft.

The elevator operator formerly was a fireman at the building, it was stated. He was working "extra" on the elevators.

Mrs. Blake was a widow. She lived with her parents, Mr. and Mrs. Charles Mount, 1420 Virginia Street. Besides her parents, she is survived by a son, Herwitt, 3 years old, a brother, William Mount, 1243 Penn street, and six sisters, one of them Mrs. Edward Stamm, 1420 Virginia Street. — Kansas City Times Wednesday.

Thursday morning's Times says in part: "Boyd Fulton, an office boy for the John A. Reed Printing Co. was the only witness. He explained his presence in the elevator. The door was open, he said, and Mrs. Blake was in the car. He entered and shortly after it started down, without the operator. Mrs. Blake, he said, leaped toward the door and grasped the beam supporting the door of the shaft. Her head was struck by the cage and her body turned to the top of the car. He had not touched the controller and had not seen Mrs Blake touch it."

Mrs. Blake was born and reared in Higginsville and had many friends here. Mrs. Fred Newman and Mrs. R. M. Sebastian of Higginsville are sisters of Mrs. Blake, as are Mrs. Fred Morgan and Mrs. James Jones of Corder. The other sister is Mrs W. B. Harris of Smithville.

The body was brought to Higginsville Thursday. The funeral will be from the Second Baptist church, this, Friday, morning, conducted by the Rev. Alfred J.

Higginsville Advance, May 19, 1916 (additional story, quotes the Kansas City Star)

Mrs. Nona Blake, 24 years old, was fatally injured by an elevator on the sixth floor of the Graphic Arts Building, Tenth and Wyandotte streets, Kansas City, Tuesday. She was a widow and leaves a 3 year-old son. The deceased was born in Higginsville.

The Concordian, May 25, 1916.

In Kansas City ist am Dienstag die vermittwete Frau Nona Blake, geb. Mount, Tochter des früher in Higginsville wohnhaften Chas. Mount, durch einen Elevator = Unfall um's Leben gekommen.

A German newspaper, Warrenton Volksfreund, May 26, 1916:
"In Kansas City, on Tuesday Mrs. Nona Blake, née Mount, daughter of Charles Mount, formerly living in Higginsville, died in an elevator accident."

CHAPTER 10

1916-1919
Kansas City, Missouri
Los Angeles, California

Kansas City

Nothing would ever be right, or normal again. That is how the families of Kansas City felt in the months after the fatal accident of May 16, 1916.

The body of Nona Lenora Mount-Blake was taken to the home of her sister, Belle Mount-Sebastian, in Higginsville on Thursday, and the funeral service and burial took place on Friday, May 19, 1916. She was laid to rest in Higginsville City Cemetery and a simple stone was placed at the gravesite that reads, "Nora Blake."

Elevator tragedies continued to happen throughout the United States and, slowly, safety precautions were implemented. But these precautions were not in place in time for Nona. There was no making sense of it, and no ability for the family to accept what had happened. They were not alone in his. The memory of Nona left a mark on the hearts of all Kansas City residents, especially when another elevator accident occurred nearly a year later.

On March 17, 1917, a man named Roy Severance was at the Graphic Arts Building and boarded an elevator. It happened to be the same car that Nona Mount-Blake had been fatally injured in. At the time Mr. Severance was in the car, an "extra man" was operating the lift. This man had no experience or qualifications to operate elevators. A malfunction occurred, and Mr. Severance's foot was caught and crushed between the elevator and the shaft.

FOOT CRUSHED BY AN ELEVATOR

Roy Severance Injured in Graphic Arts Building Shaft.

Roy Severance, 205 Monroe Avenue, an employee of the Kansas City Railways Company, suffered a crushed foot in an elevator accident at the Graphic Arts Building, Tenth and Wyandotte streets, yesterday afternoon. The accident occurred in the same car which killed Mrs. Nona Blake last May. At that time it was being operated by an "extra" man George L. Wallace, in the office of Pratt & Thompson, agents for the building, said this afternoon experienced operators only are now employed.

Severance could not explain exactly how the accident happened. As the elevator was passing one of the floors his foot was caught between the elevator and the shaft. He is not sure whether the door was closed.

Kansas City Star, March 18, 1917

The *Kansas City Star* reported on this accident, above. Per this report, as of the afternoon of March 18, 1917, "experienced operators only are now employed." This would be a step in the right direction until national safety standards were implemented in 1925. The real tragedy, however, is that Pratt-Thompson implemented subsequent remedial measures---employing only "experienced operators"—only after the death of Nona Blake and another near-fatal accident.

Though subsequent remedial measures could not be used to prove Pratt-Thompson's liability, they certainly could demonstrate that it was possible to have prevented these accidents with safer conditions in place.[1]

The Mount-Harris-Sebastian families would never recover from the loss of Nona. And yet, they all had to move on. If not for her sake, then for the sake of her son, Hurwitt.[2]

Charles and Samantha Mount took on the role of raising their grandson. In time, Frank Hurwitt Blake would learn that he had lost both his mother and father, but he would grow very close to his grandfather and his other relatives. In 1917, Charles and Samantha would take Frank to Algert T. Peterson's photography studio in Higginsville to have his portrait taken. Charles and Samantha would have their portrait taken as well. Frank spent a great deal of time with the Harrises as well and would (as Nona and Anna had hoped) grow up with his cousin, Howard B. Harris. After the deaths of his parents, Frank was adopted by Warren B. Harris and Anna Mount-Harris.

The U.S. was pulled into World War I in 1917, when President Wilson declared war on Germany on April 6, 1917. Men across the nation completed their draft registration cards including Warren B. Harris, Guy P. Sauvain, Frank J. Stamm, Algert T. Peterson, and countless others residing in Missouri. All of these men were safely at home following the war's end in 1918.

---

[1] This concept derives from Federal Rule of Evidence, Rule 407, which provides that subsequent remedial measures cannot be used to prove a party's wrongdoing or culpable conduct, but evidence of a subsequent remedial measure can be admissible for some other relevant purpose, such as to prove ownership, or control, or that it was possible to have prevented the accident with safer conditions. As there were no federal standards re: elevator safety in 1917, this would not have applied. However, once the A17 became nationally adopted in the latter twentieth century, companies like Pratt-Thompson would have been required to comply and protect against future accidents.

[2] Please see Appendix for additional news clippings about the families and photos.

Guy P. Sauvain registered for the draft on June 17, 1917 as a married man. He had married Edna Mount on April 17, 1917. Guy and Edna would have a long and happy life together in Missouri and Kansas. Guy would become an integral part of the Mount family and would make frequent visits to Kansas City to spend time with Charles Mount and Frank Hurwitt Blake. He would work in the shoe business for his entire career, managing several shoe businesses in the state of Kansas. He and Edna would move to Salina, Kansas in 1919.

The Harrises would move back to Kansas City in 1920. They would reside on Askew Ave. together with Charles Mount, Samantha Mount, and Frank H. Blake. Warren B. Harris sold the *Smithville Democrat-Herald* to Smithville postmaster Collins Kindred in December 1918. He continued to work at numerous printing establishments in Kansas City for his entire career. Son Howard B. Harris would attend Central Middle School and Central High School in Kansas City. He worked in the newspaper business alongside Warren B. Harris, but also had a keen interest in music and horseback riding. During high school, he joined Kansas City's "Tom Mix & the Pinto Band," riding horses and playing clarinet. As an adult in 1934, he worked as a lithographer in a printing office. His father W.B. worked as a pressman for the Allen Stamp Seal & Manufacturing Company at that time.

Frank Hurwitt Blake would grow up well-loved by his family, and he would excel at school. He would attend East High School in Kansas City and serve as the "Sergeant-at-Arms" for the Orchestra Club. He would also join the R.O.T.C and enlist in the U.S. Navy during World War II. Prior to the war, Hurwitt would attend law school at Kansas City School of Law, part of the 1934 graduating class. He would not practice law, but rather would use his law degree to pursue a career in real estate.

Edwin Forrest Livesay worked as a printer for Breeders Printing Company in Kansas City in the years after leaving the *Smithville Democrat-Herald*. He and spouse Edith Sebastian-Livesay had a son, Robert, in 1921. In April 1929, Edwin suffered a duodenal (abdominal) ulcer and was admitted to the Veterans Hospital in Kansas City on April 9th. Medical intervention could not save him, and he passed away on April 10th. Edith Livesay remained in Kansas City, raising their two children. She never remarried.

The Mount-Harris-Sebastian families and their descendants would remain close across the generations. Many would continue to reside in Missouri and neighboring Kansas. They forged an enduring and unbreakable bond in the years of Kansas City's substantial political and social development. From 1908 through 1920, the families endured great joy and loss in a city that was largely controlled by the newspapers and the press. The Graphic Arts Building was a symbol of this influence, representing the entire commercial printing industry and its key players: Pratt-Thompson, Campbell-Gates, and the Graphic Arts Organization itself.

There were other giants in the newspaper business, like William "Bill" Nelson of the *Kansas City Star*, Lee Shippey of the *Higginsville Jeffersonian*, and Warren B. Harris of the *Smithville Democrat-Herald*. These men impacted the lives of families living in and around Kansas City, and to a large extent, controlled the narrative of these cities and its inhabitants.

Los Angeles

The tragedy of Nona Mount-Blake was not reported in the Los Angeles, California papers. The news did reach Los Angeles, however, in late May of 1916.

Charles A. Blake had mailed a letter to the Mounts of Kansas City in March 1916, inquiring as to the well-being of Nona Mount-Blake and Frank H. Blake. Enclosed with the letter was the monthly amount Charles sent for Frank's care and education. Charles and his father, J. H. Blake, continued to receive substantial incomes from their work in the fishing industry. In 1917, San Pedro, California was known as "fish harbor," and hundreds of people relocated there for work. According to one San Pedro resident, "everybody that I knew, and everybody that I still know that worked in the fishing industry---I don't think there's a poor person around."[3]

---

[3] Mark Karmelich interview in Port of Los Angeles, "The Smell of Money: The Story of the Fishing and Canning Industry of the Los Angeles Harbor Area." March 21, 2024. Documentary, 32:05. https://www.youtube.com/watch?v=D_Fzv6T6YWk.

When Charles mailed that letter in March 1916, he reflected on his life since he had left Kansas City in 1913. He and his family had done very well for themselves, and he imagined, just for a moment, how things would be if Nona and Frank had joined him. He wondered what would have happened if Warren B. Harris had not interfered, and Nona had been free to make her own choices. He had always wanted to provide for Nona and his son, and now, as a fisherman, he could. He imagined, just for a moment, that Nona and Frank would come to California, and they could become a proper family.

But that would never be.

When Charles received a note from Kansas City informing him of Nona Mount-Blake's death, he was shattered. His entire life, and the reason he had strived to become successful in his new career, was shattered into a thousand pieces.

In one dreadful moment, his dreams of reuniting with his wife and son vanished into smoke. The only thing that kept him from collapsing was the knowledge that his son, Frank Hurwitt Blake, was alive and well and being cared for by the Mounts. Mr. Charles Mount had the kindness to communicate this to Charles, and to let him know that the money was appreciated.

So, Charles continued to send money to the Mount household. But his energy and health declined in the months following Nona's death. He began to experience fatigue and shortness of breath, especially after being out on fishing trips. At times, he felt his heart skipping. He attributed this to the grief he still felt. It was a grief that refused to dissipate, regardless of how much time passed. The fatigue and chest pain he felt was continuous, and he merely tried to move on and ignore it.

In those latter six months of 1916, the only person who distracted him from everything was Evelyn Miller. She was fourteen years old and blossoming into a lovely young woman. She had a sweetness and innocence about life, and about the world, that was endearing to Charles. She enjoyed walking the shoreline and searching for crabs, and she spoke about things that lightened his mood. She talked about the other girls in her school who won the spelling bee, and of going shopping with her mother to buy a new dress, and of the new ice-cream flavors she wished to try when the truck came by. And she put up with his moods, and was always kind to him, even when he became frustrated on days he failed to make a good catch of mackerel. "You'll go out tomorrow and catch some good ones," she would say, and then change the subject.

During this time, everyone in Redondo and San Pedro continued to inquire why Charles Blake did not have a wife. He was quite the eligible bachelor, and there were many young women who had fruitlessly vied for his attention. But Charles did not have an interest in any of them. He had decided, long ago, that he would never marry again.

But Charles was growing to appreciate Evelyn's company, and the two spent more and more time together. Charles began to think about the value of that companionship, and what it would mean to have someone like Evelyn in his life on a more permanent basis. She was the light that had drawn him out of his darkness.

In early December, Charles told his parents that he wished to propose marriage to Evelyn. Mr. and Mrs. Blake were surprised but pleased and paid a visit to the home of Mr. and Mrs. Whitney, Evelyn's parents. The Whitneys were likewise surprised but overwhelmingly in approval of the match. The success of the Blakes in the fishing industry guaranteed that their daughter would be well-provided for and would want for nothing. With that settled, all that remained was for Charles to speak with Evelyn.[4]

---

[4] William H. Miller married Kathryn Wilson about 1902 in Pennsylvania and had one daughter, Evelyn Miller. William passed before 1910, leaving Kathryn a widow. Kathryn (Wilson) Miller married Willard W. Whitney on September 25, 1916 in Los Angeles. Thus, Evelyn Miller's parents are the "Whitneys."

He did so that afternoon during their stroll along the Strand. He told her that he thought they made good companions, and then asked how she would feel about always keeping one another company. When Evelyn expressed that she would like this very much, Charles asked how she would feel about being married to him. He added that both their parents had given their approval. Evelyn liked Charles very much, and clearly her parents did as well. She thus could think of no reason against marrying Charles, so she accepted.

On Tuesday, December 19, 1916, Los Angeles County issued a marriage license to Charles A. Blake and Evelyn I. Miller. The *Los Angeles Evening Express* published this in the "Vital Statistics—Licenses to Wed" section of the December 20, 1916 issue. The paper reported Evelyn Miller's age as eighteen, which was the age of consent to marry in California.[5] Evelyn was born in 1903 and the U.S. Federal Census for 1920 lists her as seventeen years old. She would have been allowed to marry Charles in 1916 with her parents' consent.

Vital Statistics

Marriages, Births, Deaths

LICENSES TO WED

The following marriage licenses have been issued since the last publication of the list in this newspaper, the residence of the parties being Los Angeles unless otherwise given. Ages.
Steven A. Emptage, Josephine Rain.... 26—19
James J. O'Brien, Mae Koenig.......... 34—24
Joseph Betz, Lora D. Harold........... 38—35
Charles A. Blake, Evelyn I. Miller...... 26—18

---

[5] Mary E. Odom, " 'White Slaves' and 'Vicious Men': The Age of Consent Campaign" in *Delinquent Daughters: Protecting and Policing Adolescent Female Sexuality in the United States, 1885-1920* (Univ of North Carolina Press, 2000): 14.

The *Redondo Reflex* announced the Blake-Miller nuptials in its December 29, 1916 issue, stating:

> A marriage that came as a surprise to their many friends was the ceremony performed between Evelyn Miller, daughter of Mrs. W.W. Whitney, and Charles Blake, occurring in Los Angeles on Tuesday of last week at high noon. Reverend Myers officiated. Both young people are well known in Redondo Beach. Honoring the newlyweds: Mr. and Mrs. J.H. Blake and Mr. and Mrs. W.W. Whitney entertained with a turkey dinner at Hotel Redondo last Sunday and covers were laid for twelve.

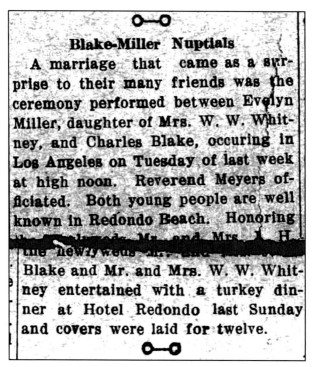

Charles A. Blake thus began the year 1917 as a man with a wife, and a son. He eventually told Evelyn about his prior marriage to Nona Mount and her death, but never disclosed that he had a son in Kansas City, Missouri. He continued to send money to the Mounts discreetly, and Evelyn was none the wiser.

State of California   County of Los Angeles

Marriage License

These Presents Are to authorize and license any Justice of the Supreme Court, Justice of the District Court of Appeal, Judge of the Superior Court, Justice of the Peace, Judge of any Police Court, City Recorder, Priest or Minister of the Gospel of any denomination, to solemnize within said County the marriage of *Charley A. Blake* a native of *Iowa* {Color or Race} Caucasian aged *26* years, resident of *Redondo Beach*, County of *Los Angeles* State of California, and *Evelyn S. Miller*, a native of *Penna* {Color or Race} Caucasian aged *18* years, resident of *Redondo Beach*, County of *Los Angeles*, State of California, said parties being of sufficient age to be capable of contracting marriage.

In **Witness Whereof** I have hereunto set my hand, and affixed the seal of the Superior [SEAL] Court of said County, this *19* day of *Dec* A.D. 1916

H. J. LELANDE,

County Clerk, and ex-officio Clerk of the Superior Court in and for said Los Angeles County.

By *R. S. Banks* Deputy Clerk

STATE OF CALIFORNIA, } ss.   I hereby certify, that I believe the facts stated in the within and above License to be true, County of Los Angeles,

and that upon due inquiry, there appears to be no legal impediment to the marriage of said *Charles A. Blake* and *Evelyn S. Miller* that said parties were joined in marriage by me on the *19* day of *Dec* 1916, in *Los Angeles* said County and State; that *Mrs Ada Blake* a resident of *Redondo Beach*, County of *Los Angeles*, State of *Calif* and , a resident of , County of State of was present as witness of said ceremony.

I have hereunto set my hand this *19* day of *Dec* A.D. 1916

James S. Myers

Signature of party performing ceremony.

Minister

Title

6600

A full, true and correct copy of the original, recorded this *27* day of *Dec* 1916, at 5 P.M.

at request of *Minister*

C. L. LOGAN, County Recorder

By *C. E. Young* Deputy

California State Board of Health

PLACE OF MARRIAGE

BUREAU OF VITAL STATISTICS

State Index No.

County of Los Angeles

Certificate of Marriage

Town of

Local Register No. *6682*

City of

PERSONAL AND STATISTICAL PARTICULARS

	GROOM		BRIDE	
FULL NAME	*Charles A. Blake*		*Evelyn S. Miller*	
RESIDENCE	*Redondo Beach Cal*		*Redondo Beach, Cal.*	
AGE AT LAST BIRTHDAY	*26* years		*18* years	
COLOR OR RACE	*White*		*White*	
SINGLE WIDOWED OR DIVORCED	*Widowed*		*Single*	
NUMBER OF MARRIAGE	*2nd*		*1st*	
BIRTHPLACE (State or County)	*Iowa*		*Penna*	
OCCUPATION	*Waiter*			
NAME OF FATHER	*James Blake*		*Wm. Miller*	
BIRTHPLACE OF FATHER (State or County)	*Iowa*		*Penna*	
MAIDEN NAME OF MOTHER	*Ada Snow*		*Kathryn Wilson*	
BIRTHPLACE OF MOTHER (State or County)	*Iowa*		*Penna*	

MAIDEN NAME OF THE BRIDE, IF SHE WAS PREVIOUSLY MARRIED

We, the groom and bride named in this certificate, hereby certify that the information given therein is correct, to the best of our knowledge and belief.

Groom sign here *Chas Blake*   Bride sign here *Evelyn Miller*

CERTIFICATE OF PERSON PERFORMING CEREMONY

I Hereby Certify that *Charles A. Blake* and *Evelyn S. Miller*

were joined in marriage by me in accordance with the Laws of the State of California, at *Los Angeles*

this *19* day of *Dec* 1916

Signature of Witness to the Marriage *Mrs Ada Blake*   Signature of Person Performing the Ceremony *James S. Myers*

Residence *Redondo Beach Cal.*   Official Station *Minister*

Filed *Dec 27 1916*   Residence *Los Angeles Cal*

C. L. LOGAN,

Registrar (County Recorder)

Note error on certificate under occupation. Charles was a fisherman. Evelyn was a waitress.

When the U.S. officially entered the war in April 1917, Charles applied for a Merchant Marine license to operate motorboats. The license was issued on June 27, 1917. Charles had signed his draft registration card on June 4, 1917, listing his employment as "fisherman," and his residence as "Redondo Beach." He claimed an exemption from the draft. The reason stated was, "support wife and child."

13551—Redondo Beach, Southern California, U. S. A.

WWI Draft Reg. Card for Charles A. Blake. Source: WWI Selective Service System Draft Registration Cards, 1917-1918. Washington, D.C.: NARA. M1509.

Obtaining the Merchant Marine license was thus strategic, allowing Charles to remain in California to operate motorboats in Los Angeles. At the time of completing his Merchant Marine license application, Charles' stated residence was San Pedro.

Records of the Bureau of Marine Inspection and Navigation. Merchant Marine Applications for Licenses of Officers, U.S. Merchant Marine Application for Charles A. Blake. Charles' brother Theodore also applied for the same license in August 1918.

Charles Blake thus continued to work as a motorboat operator and fisherman, supporting Evelyn and his son, and traveling where there was the greatest opportunity to make a profit. San Pedro, California was rich in these opportunities, but so was San Francisco.

San Francisco was just as prominent of a fishing port as San Pedro, and even more so in the late 1800s. By 1880, San Francisco handled more fish than all the other ports combined, including from San Diego. In 1892, the Bay Area accounted for 93% of California's commercial fishery products. The best place for sardines was San Pedro in the 1900s, while San Francisco offered sturgeon and salmon.[6]

In the winter of 1919, J.H. Blake still worked as a traveling salesman for the Morris Packing Company in addition to his work as a fisherman in Redondo Beach and San Pedro. At the age of 49, he was healthy and full of vigor, but preferred not to travel. He enjoyed staying in the Los Angeles area with his wife and sons. When a lucrative opportunity arose in San Francisco, however, he could not pass it up. He thus asked his older son, Charles, if he would make the trip.

Charles could easily manage the trip, and he was just as interested in the opportunity as his father. He agreed to go on his father's behalf. He would depart in November. His wife, Evelyn, would remain in San Pedro. He told her and his parents that he would be in the San Francisco Bay for no more than three days. It was settled.

When Charles began packing for the trip, he felt that odd and recurring chest pain and fatigue again. It was only mildly concerning to him—he had dealt with it before, and he would just wait for it to pass.

Eventually, the feeling did pass, but only until Charles arrived in San Francisco in the third week of November. He rented a room on 3rd Street, about a mile from Piers 1½ and 3. These piers were located on San Francisco's Northeast Waterfront, adjacent to the Ferry Building, and newly built in 1918.

---

[6] Love, "Subsistence, Commercial, and Recreational Fisheries" in *The Ecology of Marine Fishes: California and Adjacent Waters.*

Piers 1 ½ and 3 were used for transportation and shipping and housed a number of inland companies with workers from all manner of industries. These included wholesale packing and shipping, fishing, and steel work. They all shared a bulkhead office, warehouse spaces, and huge transit sheds.[7]

Charles had a meeting at the Piers with some associates of his father. He arrived in San Francisco on November 20, 1919, and was set to meet with the associates the next day, November 21. With any luck, he would be on his way home to San Pedro on the 22nd, in time to join his family for Thanksgiving.

This would not be the case.

Charles had arrived in San Francisco late in the day on the 20th and did not get up to his room until nearly eleven-o-clock that evening. He stayed up, looking over some papers and letters that he had brought with him. There was a letter from his parents, an old one that he had saved.

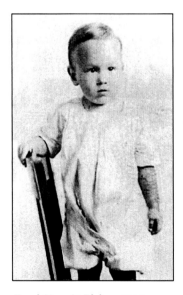

He also had the last letter from Mr. Charles Mount, which stated that Frank Hurwitt Blake was a safe, healthy, and happy child who was thriving under the Mounts' care. When Charles had initially opened the letter, he did not see the photograph that was enclosed. He had missed it amidst the shock of learning of Nona's death. Weeks later when he re-opened the letter, he saw it. It was a photograph of a beautiful little boy. It was a photograph of his son. He had it in his vest pocket on that night, and (as was his habit), he took it out to gaze at it, wondering how his son was doing and how much he had grown.

Frank Hurwitt Blake, c. 1915

[7] National Park Service, "Central Embarcadero Piers Historic District", https://www.nps.gov/places/central-embarcadero-piers-historic-district.htm; US Dep't. of Interior, National Park Service, National Register of Historic Places Registration form for Central Embarcadero Piers Historic District, Piers 1, 1 ½ , 3, 5 (submitted Oct. 8, 2002).

Charles grew tired as the clock struck thirty minutes past midnight. As he rose from the bed to change into nightclothes, a sudden severe chest pain took hold of him. He pressed his hand to his chest and instantly was seized with dizziness. He tried to sit down, and he managed to reach a cup of water from the bedside table. But his hand shook as he brought the cup to his lips, and he was again seized with a searing pain that brought him to his knees. He could not breathe, and he was blinded by the pain in his chest, the pain in his heart. He tried to call out for help, but he became so dizzy he could barely see straight. He did not know what was happening. He was completely terrified.

He vaguely became aware of distant voices, a man in uniform, bright lights and sirens, and someone saying, "emergency hospital."

Then, he was aware of nothing.

Charles A. Blake was found by the police at 1:10 a.m. and brought immediately to Central East Emergency Hospital in San Francisco. He was examined and determined to have suffered a cardiac arrest. He remained under the care and observation of James R. Clark, M.D. throughout that long night.

But there was nothing that could be done. Charles was declared deceased at 8:10 a.m. on November 21, 1919. He had suffered from chronic valvular disease for many years that had been unaddressed and untreated. He had ignored his symptoms of chest pain and fatigue. His heart ultimately failed him in those early morning hours.

He had never changed out of his day clothes. When the coroner examined him at 8:30 a.m., the following items were found on him: letters, photographs, a cigarette holder, and a comb. Among the photographs was one of a small boy labelled "Frank Hurwitt Blake."

The coroner's office discerned the names and address of Charles' parents from the letters. A telegram was sent to Mr. and Mrs. Blake, at 330 Seventh St., San Pedro, to notify them of their son's death.

James H. Blake made it to San Francisco on November 22nd to identify his son's body and to make arrangements to bring his son home. He forcefully pushed down his grief, as he knew it was most important to bring Charles back to Los Angeles where he could have a proper burial.

The Blake family held a funeral service for their son Charles on Monday, November 24, 1919, in Los Angeles, officiated by Reverend T. J. Oliver Curran. Charles' body was cremated following the service.

> **NEW GAS CONNECTIONS**
> **San Pedro**
> Hellen Anderson, 316 N. Mesa.
> T. H. Nemec, 571 Sepulveda.
> Mrs. J. H. Blake, 330 W. Seventh.
> Fred Dahn, 291 W. Sixth.

Clipping from San Pedro News Pilot, October 1, 1919, confirming the Blakes' address at 330 W. Seventh St.

> Charles A. Blake, aged 30 years, son of James Blake of 330 Seventh street, died yesterday at the Central Emergency hospital in San Francisco. The body was cremated in Los Angeles this afternoon in charge of R. S. Goodrich.

San Pedro Daily Pilot, November 24, 1919

The body of the late Charles A. Blake of Vail, Iowa, was cremated yesterday in Los Angeles. Rev. T. J. Oliver Curran officiated at the funeral service preceding the cremation. The deceased died in San Francisco November 21 and was born April 20, 1890. He leaves to mourn his loss his wife, parents and a sister, Mrs. H. L. Croy of Tuscon, Ariz., a brother, Theodore R. Blake, of this city. He was a member of the Episcopal church.

San Pedro Daily Pilot, November 25, 1919

Note: the death certificate lists Charles Blake's occupation as steel worker. This may be inaccurate, as other sources indicate that Charles continued to work as a fisherman and that his primary residence was San Pedro, CA.

DEATH REPORT, CORONER'S OFFICE

Date Received *Nov. 21–1919* Time Received, *8.30 am*

Name of Person Reporting Case, *Central E. Hospital*

Address " " "   Tel. No.

Name of Deceased, *Charles A. Blake*

CHARLES A. BLAKE

Male — Female   Color, *White*

Age, *M 30*   Nativity, *Iowa*

Married or Single   Occupation, *Iron Worker*

Residence, *149–3rd st*

Place Where Death Occurred, *Central E. Hospital*

Time of Death or }
When Found Dead }   *8.10. am Nov 21–1919.*

Presumable Cause of Death, *Cardiac disease*

Body Received at Morgue *9.35. Am Nov 21–1919.*

Deputy, *M. Brown.* Messenger *F. Alvesahl.*

Undertaker, *Halstead & Co. from Nov 21–19 2 P.M.*

Order for Burial Signed by

Relation to Deceased   **HALSTEAD & CO. FUNERAL HOME**

Certificate Sent to Board of Health

IN CASE OF ACCIDENT, SUICIDE, ETC., INFORMATION PRIOR TO TIME OF DEATH

Time of Accident or Suicide,

Place of Accident or Suicide,

Nature of Accident or Suicide,

When Received in Hospital, *Nov 21– 1.10 am*

Predisposing Cause, if Suicide,

CHARLES A. BLAKE, AGE 29, AUTOPSY REPORT

AUTOPSY CERTIFICATE   San Francisco, *Nov. 21,*   19 *19*

I hereby certify that I have made an autopsy or examination of the body of

mentioned above, on this *21* day of *Nov.* 19 *19*

at *9.35* o'clock, *A.* M., and that the cause of death is

Chronic Valvular disease of the General Dropsy.

CHRONIC VALVULAR DISEASE OF THE HEART, GENERAL DROPSY

John R. Clark M. D.

Death report from the coroner's office.

Date _Nov 21_____19_19_

PROPERTY

No. Property
Clothes Locker # 3
The clothing was searches at the coroner and the
following *letter* was found
Letters
Photographs
Cigarette Holder
Comb

Telegram sent to 330 7th St San Pedro

Certificate to _____Undertaker 11/21/19. 2ⁿᵈ P.M.

The Above Property Delivered by
Deputy   19   and Received by
Remains Delivered by   19

WITNESSES

NAME	ADDRESS	WHAT THEY KNOW
Police officer J. Miles. Central P. station		
heart.		

Signature of person receiving report,

Death report from the coroner's office, continued.

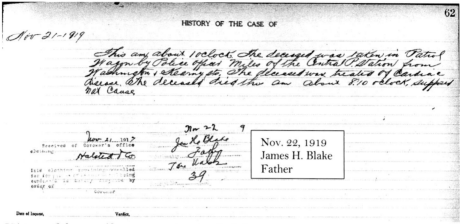

History of the case (from coroner's report) states:
This a.m. about 1-o-clock the deceased was taken in Patrol Wagon by Police Officer
Miles of the Central Police Station from Washington & Kearney Streets. The deceased
was treated of cardiac disease. The deceased died this a.m. about 8:10-o-clock, supposed
natural causes.

There was no ability for the Blakes to fully process and accept their son's death.
Like Nona Mount-Blake, Charles A. Blake had died too soon and too young,
leaving a large extended family to mourn.

Young Evelyn was a widow at age sixteen. Following Charles' death, she had
no need or desire to remain in San Pedro. She moved with her parents and
brother to El Segundo, California and found work as a waitress. Some years
later, she met James A. Kelley, a truck driver from Terminal, California, also
known as Terminal Island. They married on November 6, 1925. Evelyn was 23
years old, and James was 26.

Marriage license for James A. Kelly and Evelyn Blake.

DO NOT WRITE ON THIS SIDE

ALL BLANKS BELOW ARE FOR USE OF COUNTY RECORDER

☞ SEE FULL INSTRUCTIONS ☜

1 PLACE OF MARRIAGE	California State Board of Health BUREAU OF VITAL STATISTICS	State Index No. _____
County of Los Angeles	STANDARD CERTIFICATE OF MARRIAGE PERSONAL AND STATISTICAL PARTICULARS	Local Registered No. 13846
GROOM		BRIDE

GROOM	BRIDE
1 FULL NAME James A. Kelly	14 FULL NAME Evelyn I. Blake
2 RESIDENCE 243 Seaside Ave., Terminal, Cal.	15 RESIDENCE 601 W. Grand Ave., El Segundo, Cal.
4 COLOR OR RACE White	5 AGE AT LAST BIRTHDAY 26 (Years)	16 COLOR OR RACE White	17 AGE AT LAST BIRTHDAY 23 (Years)
6 SINGLE WIDOWED OR DIVORCED Single	7 NUMBER OF MARRIAGE 1st	18 SINGLE WIDOWED OR DIVORCED Widowed	19 NUMBER OF MARRIAGE 2nd
8 BIRTHPLACE (State or country) N. Y.	20 BIRTHPLACE (State or country) Penna.
9 OCCUPATION (a) Trade, profession, or particular kind of work Truck Driver	21 OCCUPATION (a) Trade, profession, or particular kind of work ---
(b) General nature of industry, business, or establishment in which employed (or employer) ---	(b) General nature of industry, business, or establishment in which employed (or employer) ---
10 NAME OF FATHER John Kelly	22 NAME OF FATHER Wm. H. Miller
11 BIRTHPLACE OF FATHER (State or country) N. Y.	23 BIRTHPLACE OF FATHER (State or country) Penna.
12 MAIDEN NAME OF MOTHER Lena Bach	24 MAIDEN NAME OF MOTHER Kathryn H. Wilson
13 BIRTHPLACE OF MOTHER (State or country) N. Y.	25 BIRTHPLACE OF MOTHER (State or country) Penna.

26 MAIDEN NAME OF BRIDE, IF SHE WAS PREVIOUSLY MARRIED ----

WE, the groom and bride named in this Certificate, hereby certify that the information given therein is correct, to the best of our knowledge and belief.

James A. Kelly   27 Groom   Evelyn I. Blake   28 Bride

CERTIFICATE OF PERSON PERFORMING CEREMONY

I HEREBY CERTIFY that   James A. Kelly   and
Evelyn I. Blake   *were joined in marriage by me*

in accordance with the laws of the State of California, at Los Angeles

this 6th *day of* November 19 25

31 Signature of Witness to the Marriage George W. J. Olds	Signature of Person Performing the Ceremony Walter S. Gates
Residence 536 Echo Park Ave., L. A.	Official position Judge of Superior Court
32 FILED NOV 9 1925 C. L. LOGAN, Recorder, Registrar (County Recorder)	Residence Los Angeles, Cal.

A full, true and correct copy of the original recorded this 9th *day of* November 1925, *at 9 A. M.*

C. L. LOGAN, Recorder,

By *M. A. Ryan* Deputy

NOTICE: DO NOT WRITE ON THIS PAGE
ALL BLANKS ABOVE ARE FOR THE RECORDER'S USE

Census records indicate that Evelyn Blake and James Kelley were married at least until 1930. The 1930 U. S. Census taken on April 13, 1930, shows Evelyn Kelly (age 28) as the married Head of Household, employed as a waitress, and renting her home for $25/month, at 339 North Pacific Avenue, San Pedro Dist., City of Los Angeles, Los Angeles Co., CA.

The 1940 U. S. Census taken on April 27, 1940, shows James Kelly (age 41) as an unmarried Blister Rust Laborer for the W. P. A., and living in El Dorado Co., CA.

James and Ada Blake remained in Los Angeles, California. They had never left since first relocating there from Missouri in 1913. James eventually retired from the fishing and wholesale industries and took up work as a custodian in his later years. Likely, he had accumulated substantial wealth in fishing that he had no need to work.

James would pass away in 1953 at the age of 83. His spouse, Ada, would predecease him in 1941 at the age of 75. Both James and Ada resided in San Diego at the time of their deaths. They were buried at Rose Hills Memorial Park in Los Angeles County.

Life would thus continue in Los Angeles County. Even Higginsville, Missouri newspaper man Lee Shippey would relocate to Los Angeles in 1920 and become a prominent writer for the *Los Angeles Times.*

Life would also continue in Missouri for the descendants of the Mount, Sebastian, and Harris families, as well as for Frank Hurwitt Blake. Frank would marry Lorraine Alsace Derby in 1932 and they would have two daughters, Sharon Blake and Michele Blake.

Howard B. Harris and his wife Agnes would go on to have three children: Howard B. Harris, Jr. (1937), Sandra K. Harris (1940), and Marci A. Harris (1945).

AFTERWORD

This book is a tribute to Nona Mount-Blake. It is also a tribute to the early years of Kansas City, Missouri and surrounding areas, and the people and institutions that shaped those areas. The Mount, Sebastian, Harris, and Sauvain families, and many other families, were integral to the culture and development of Kansas City and Higginsville and left an enduring legacy.

This book is a result of extensive research on these families and the Kansas City area in the early twentieth century, as derived from resources including the National Archives & Records Administration; records preserved on the ancestry.com and newspapers.com databases; the Library of Congress; the State Historical Society of Missouri; the Kansas City Public Library; and secondary books and journal articles. These resources helped to construct the historical background for this book.

The narrative and intricate family details are the result of archived documents and family stories that have been passed down across the generations. Warren B. Harris' complex relationship with Charles A. Blake is one such story that has been told and preserved.

The Missouri newspapers, 1900-1980, archived on newspapers.com and the State Historical Society of Missouri, also had a significant role in shaping this book. The papers shared news and stories in a manner that was strategic and often driven by politics. The frequent mentions of Lee Shippey and W.B. Harris in Missouri newspapers, for example, indicate their prominent voice and presence. The characterization of elevator fatalities as "accidents," and the rigorous promotion of Dress-Up week are examples of social politics at work. The myriad of newspaper articles included in this book thus are intended to complement the story and bring the history of the time period to life.

The California newspapers had a like purpose. Not much was known about the Blake family in the early twentieth century after the family moved away from Missouri. The local Redondo Beach newspaper, the *Redondo Reflex*, helped to fill in the gaps, from James H. Blake's success as a fisherman to how Charles A. Blake met Evelyn I. Miller. The Blakes' life and success in Los Angeles also serves the larger purpose of shining light on the fishing industry and its huge impact on cities like San Pedro, Redondo Beach, and San Francisco.

These stories will be forever preserved in the archived newspapers. It is my intent that the families behind these stories are honored and preserved here.

Top: postcard depicting Kansas City, 1910s; bottom: glass negative of Main Street in Higginsville, 1910s.

APPENDIX

Photographs & Newspaper Clippings

❖

The Mount and Blake families; Frank Hurwitt Blake

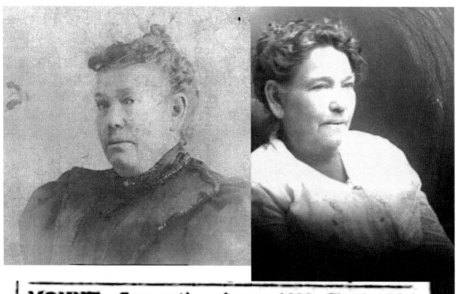

MOUNT—Samantha Ann, 4408 East 24th
st., passed away at the age of 70 years.
Surviving are her husband, Charles S.
Mount of the home address; 1 son, William Mount of Kansas City; 6 daughters.
Mrs. R. M. Sebastian, Mrs. Fred Newman
of Higginsville, Mo.; Mrs. Fred Morgan,
Corder, Mo.; Mrs. G. P. Souvain, Hutchin-
son, Kas.; Mrs. W. B. Harris, Mrs. J. E.
Ronk of Kansas City. Burial at Higginsville, Mo. Taylor funeral home.

*Kansas City Journal, November 27, 1927, listing Samantha Mount's son and
daughters. Belle Mount married R.M. Sebastian; Stella Mount married Fred
Newman; Elizabeth Mount married Fred Morgan; Edna Mount married G.P.
Sauvain; Anna Mount married W.B. Harris; and Mamie Mount married John
Ronk.*

Glass negatives taken by A.T. Peterson at his studio in Higginsville, MO, c. 1917

Charles & Samantha Mount; Frank H. Blake

Frank Hurwitt Blake with grandfather Charles S. Mount, July 1921, Kansas City

Commercial Club 2; Ag. Club 3; Home Econo-
mics Club 1: Choral Club 1-2-3; German Club
4; Sport Editor Echo Staff 4; Music Contest
1-2-3.

FRANCES SCHWARTZ
"Happy. carefree and gav."
G. H. S. C. 1-2; Ag. Club 4, Choral Club 2-
3-4; Science Club 3.

HURWITT BLAKE
*"A cheerful grin will let you in, where the
kicker is never known."*
R. O. T. C., Sergeant 4: Band 2-3-4; Asst.
Director 4; Treasurer 3-4; Orchestra 3-4;
Sgt.-at-Arms 4; Senior Day Committee.

East High School yearbook photo, 1930

RAYMOND E. BEGGS
2302 Central
Kansas City, Kansas.

FRANK H. BLAKE
2940 Askew.
Independent Club.

Kansas City School of Law yearbook photo, 1934

Portrait of Lorraine Alsace Derby, Frank H. Blake's wife (married 1932);

WWII draft registration card for Frank Hurwitt Blake. He was living in Kansas City with wife Lorraine and working for Business Mens Assurance Co.

SERIAL NUMBER	1. NAME (Print)			ORDER NUMBER
543	FRANK (First)	HURWITT (Middle)	BLAKE (Last)	2315

2. ADDRESS (Print) 5834 Jackson
3011 Cypress Kansas City Jackson Mo
(Number and street or R. F. D. number) (Town) (County) (State)

3. TELEPHONE	4. AGE IN YEARS	5. PLACE OF BIRTH	6. COUNTRY OF CITIZENSHIP
	27	Kansas City	
WA. 3017	DATE OF BIRTH Jan. 5 1913	Town or county Mo.	U. S. A.
(Exchange) (Number)	(Mo.) (Day) (Yr.)	(State or country)	

7. NAME OF PERSON WHO WILL ALWAYS KNOW YOUR ADDRESS
Mrs Lorraine Alsace Blake
(Mr., Mrs., Miss) (First) (Middle) (Last)

8. RELATIONSHIP OF THAT PERSON Wife

9. ADDRESS OF THAT PERSON
3011 Cypress Kansas City Jackson Mo
(Number and street or R. F. D. number) (Town) (County) (State)

10. EMPLOYER'S NAME
Business Mens Assurance Co

11. PLACE OF EMPLOYMENT OR BUSINESS
215 Pershing Rd. K. C. Jackson Mo
(Number and street or R. F. D. number) (Town) (County) (State)

I AFFIRM THAT I HAVE VERIFIED ABOVE ANSWERS AND THAT THEY ARE TRUE.

REGISTRATION CARD
D. S. S. Form 1 (over) 16—17105 (Registrant's signature)

CHARLES S. MOUNT DIES.

In 1865 He Was Fireman on One of First Trains Through Here.

Charles S. Mount died yesterday at the home of a daughter, Mrs. W. B. Harris, 2940 Askew avenue. He would have been 92 years old Memorial day.

Born in Montgomery, Ala., Mount served as a private in the Missouri Home guard at St. Louis in the last years of the Civil war. He was fireman on one of the first Missouri Pacific trains to come through here when the main line was put down in 1865. Later he was a hoisting engineer for many years in the coal fields near Higginsville. He was a charter member of the Odd Fellows' lodge at Higginsville.

Surviving also are five other daughters, Mrs. R. M. Sebastian and Mrs. S. R. Smith, of Corder, Mo.; Mrs. Fred Newman of Higginsville; Mrs. G. P. Sauvain of Salina, Kas., and Mrs. Mame Runk, Chesterfield hotel, and a son, William Mount, 3929 Forest avenue.

Charles S. Mount in MO, 1929;
Obit for Charles S. Mount printed in Kansas City Times, April 10, 1941;
Headstone for Charles & Samantha Mount, Higginsville City Cemetery

> **Mr. and Mrs. Frank H. Blake, 823 West Seventy-seventh street, announce the birth, November 24, of a daughter whom they have named Sharon.**

Kansas City Times, December 5, 1939

> ## DIXIE KIEFER POST ELECTS.
>
> ### Frank H. Blake Heads the American Legion Unit.
>
> Frank H. Blake, 27 East Pocahontas lane, has been elected commander of the Dixie Kiefer post of the American Legion. He succeeds Miles Gaynes, who was elected delegate to the city central committee.

Kansas City Times, August 20, 1948. The American Legion is a veterans' organization. Frank H. Blake was a WWII veteran, having served in the U.S. Navy aboard the USS Carlisle. See below muster roll.

of U. S. S. CARLISLE (APA 69) 30th day of MAY , 19 45, date of sailing from Navy # 128 to Navy #24						
1 NAMES (Alphabetically arranged without regard to ratings, with surname to the left and the first name written in full)	**2** SERVICE NUMBER (The service number must under no condition be omitted)	**3** Rating at Date of Last Report	**4** Date of Enlistment			**5** Place of Enlistment
			Day	Mo.	Yr.	
1 BLAKE, Frank Hurwitt	989019	Private	29	5	44	Kansas City, Mo

Risk Official Buys Store.

Frank H. Blake, 9708 Belleview, has purchased the Buck Creek store on state road O, near Gravois Mills, Mo. Blake, who has been with the Business Men's Assurance company 31 years, served as assistant treasurer the last 14 years.

He will move today and begin operation of the store tomorrow. He will be assisted by his wife Lorraine, a daughter Michelle; another daughtter, Sharon, and Sharon's husband, Frank Carter. The Blakes have had a cottage in this area for a year.

Blake eventually plans to enter the insurance and real estate business in the Gravois Mills area.

Kansas City Star, September 1, 1961

FRANK H. BLAKE

Frank Hurwitt Blake, 68, Versailles, Mo., formerly of Kansas City, died Thursday at a nursing home in Versailles. He was born in Kansas City and had lived in this area most of his life before moving to Versailles in 1960. Mr. Blake was a real estate agent for the Russell P. Hall Real Estate Co., Laurie, Mo., 20 years. He previously had been assistant treasurer of Business Men's Assurance Company of America. He was a past commander of the Dixie Kiefer American Legion Post, Kansas City, and a former Chef de Guerre of the Forty and Eight Society, Kansas City. He was a Marine Corps veteran of World War II. He leaves his wife, Mrs. Lorraine Blake of the home; two daughters, Mrs. Michele Miller, Versailles, and Mrs. Sharon Carter, Kansas City; and three granddaughters. Memorial services will be at 11 a.m. Saturday at the Kidwell-Garber Chapel, Versailles; cremation.

Obit for Frank Hurwitt Blake, Kansas City Times, Dec. 25, 1981

The Los Angeles Blakes

Redondo Reflex, December 18, 1914, pg. 1

NIGHT OF TERROR ON RAGING OCEAN

LAUNCH OF J. H. BLAKE DRIFTS SEAWARD IN STORM

"SAVED BY THE GRACE OF GOD!"

Men and Women Pass an Appalling Experience, During Which Hope Seemed Useless Thing

Thrilling experiences in a near-tragedy at sea, Wednesday, aboard their twenty-foot motor boat "Cutter," which drifted fifteen miles beyond the channel, driven before a sixty-mile gale and in a record-breaking rain, are being recounted by J. H. Blake and family and two young girls, who survived the terrible ordeal against odds that only the Infinite Preserver could overcome.

The happy party, which left Wednesday morning about 10 o'clock for Rocky Point, to get abalones, was composed of J. H. Blake, wholesale man for the Morris Packing Company, Los Angeles; Mrs. Blake and the daughter, Mrs. Harold Croy, and the sons, Charles Blake, aged 25, and Theodore, aged about 12; Ruth Smith, fourteen-year-old daughter of Mr. and Mrs. Morris L. Smith; and Evelyn Miller, twelve-year-old daughter of Mr. and Mrs. Miller living in Catalina avenue.

Reached Hermosa Beach

The party was adrift at the mercy of the storm-clashing elements from about 4:30 p.m. Wednesday to near 6 o'clock Thursday morning, when, having been at anchor about two hundred yards out from the Hermosa Beach pier for near two hours, anglers saw the distress' signals, heard the shouts of the men, and in a short time had rescued the exhausted, benumbed and almost hysterical people for whom many boats had been searching the angry sea during the entire night.

Charles Shaw was the first to see the "Cutter" and give the alarm. A skiff manned by Shaw and Joe Sweeney was lowered and with much difficulty members of the party climbed the narrow iron steps which led to safety on the pier.

Brought Home in Automobile

They were conveyed at once to the home of Mr. and Mrs. Shaw and given nourishing hot drinks. When partly restored to a semblance of comfort, the Blake party was brought by machines to the home in Sunset court. Friends, anxious watchers and searchers were notified of the happy finale in an experience seldom recounted by the dramatis personae in such a harrowing scene staged upon the bosom of the Pacific. The two young girl friends, "Tooty" (Ruth) Smith and Evelyn Miller, were put to bed and Mrs. Croy endeavored to get some needed rest and quiet. Their faces were scarlet from exposure, together with nervous reaction and cook-stove heat which made the four-room cottage almost unbearably warm to callers and newspaper folk who invaded the home by 10 o'clock to get the story first-hand.

First Food in Many Hours

Mrs. Blake was having a little breakfast—the first food since the
(Continued on Page Four)

Redondo Reflex, December 18, 1914, continued

NIGHT OF TERROR ON RAGING OCEAN

(Continued From First Page)

ocean lunch Wednesday noon. She was very weak and somewhat nervous, but otherwise appeared about her usual self.

Charles Blake was obviously the most nervous and physically exhausted, his arms almost refusing to follow his bidding.

Mrs. Croy joined the family group for a while and seemed not seriously the worse for her experience. Her husband, who is on the torpedo boat "Whipple," now at San Pedro, came over yesterday afternoon to see the rescued family.

The boy Theodore had escaped the long agony endured by the others, having come in with a Mexican, Timothy Ozumiga, in the latter's own small rowboat to Redondo Beach about 5 o'clock Wednesday afternoon. They notified the fishermen and all returned to the search, blowing their foghorns. The downpour continued incessantly and the searchers returned unsuccessful about 6:30 o'clock.

The Searching Crews

On the "Moon" were Clyde Henderson, Charles Day and George Feder. The "Moon" made a second trip with the Henderson boys aboard and they, too, "stood by" without success. The "Cub," bearing Harry Mead and Arthur Day, and the "Jessie M.," with the Smith boys, twins bearing the same name (Charlie) on her, went out about 9 o'clock.

Joining in the search was the "Challenger," on which were Hans Karstensen and Charles Day. Theodore Blake accompanied one of the searching parties which returned about midnight. Through sheer exhaustion the little fellow, who is a cripple and obliged to use a crutch, had to give up and go to bed at the home of Mrs. Hebertz.

City Marshal Mosier and a company of men established headquarters at the City Hall when it was learned that report of the return of the fishing party was erroneous. Mr. Mosier 'phoned to San Pedro for a cruiser or torpedo boat with searchlight to be sent over. This was between 11 and 12 o'clock. Report came back that a torpedo boat had been sent, but a later message from San Pedro announced the boat could not start until daybreak. Two Jap boats with lights and a torpedo boat were said to be "leaving soon" when the Harbor City was called again about 4:30 a.m. Thursday. The wireless went out of commission about that time and there was no further connection from the Government station at San Pedro with the war vessels.

Redondo Reflex, December 18, 1914, continued

Experiences of Castaways

Meantime six human beings were at the mercy of the storm-tossed sea. The story was told chiefly by Mrs. Blake and son Charles and the former said:

"I never felt lost, even when we were drifting out of the channel into the sea. The first we noticed we were adrift was when lights began to disappear. Could you have seen the waves you never would have thought we could live through the experience. I prayed and prayed that the wind might abate, and we huddled under the sail which Charlie had ripped off to protect us, and that was our only shelter. We moved sometimes from one end of the boat to the other for balance, while the men baled out water.

"The children were lovely and only once did one of the little girls begin to cry softly for her mother. I said, 'Now, be a brave little woman, for I feel that we shall all be saved.' She was reassured when I said that doubtless boats were out searching and would find us. When we asked the girls how they felt, they replied, 'We feel as well as can be.' Excitement kept us all up, and I don't believe any of us felt hungry,

By Grace of Cod

"We all prayed that the storm would abate. About midnight the off-shore wind, which is so dangerous to craft at sea, and a thousand times more so to us, changed suddenly. The men held up the sail, I sat at the rudder, the girls sang, and underneath a starlight sky we drifted toward Hermosa Beach. I feel we were saved by the grace of God!"

Charlie Blake stated the "Cutter" carried duplicate parts and a full boat equipment, including eight life preservers, four of which were carried away by wind and wave. The anchor would not hold on the shale bottom in such a gale. He and the other rescued ones were grateful and happy, and thankful beyond words to express themselves for their safety.

The mother of Ruth Smith was wholly unaware of the night's near-tragedy, for she believed her daughter was home with the Blakes who would not allow her to come out in the storm. It was not until morning that she heard the story, and five minutes afterward came the report the party had been rescued.

The Blakes were seen late last evening and all members of the household appeared in about their normal condition, scarce even the traces of colds being noticed. The little girls were reading a story book and their elders were going about their usual duties. Mrs. Blake requested The Reflex to express their thanks and gratitude to the people of Redondo Beach whose efforts to rescue them, and prayers in their behalf during the night, were most deeply appreciated and would never be forgotten.

Surprise: The storm and harrowing incident the Blakes endured was also reported in fourteen Missouri newspapers.

Below: Kansas City Post, December 17, 1914. Mentions the Blake family, including Mr. & Mrs. J.H. Blake, Harriet Blake-Croy (age 17), and Charles Blake (age 22, who had been reported deceased in 1913 by W.B. Harris). Ruth Smith (age 11) and "girl chum" Evelyn Miller (age 12) mentioned.

LAUNCH WEATHERS GALE; SIX RESCUED IN SORRY PLIGHT

LOS ANGELES, Dec. 17.—After battling all night against high seas and a driving rain to keep a frail launch afloat, a woman, three girls and two men were rescued this morning.

Mr. and Mrs. J. H. Blake, Charles Blake, 22; Harriet Blake, 17; Ruth Smith, 11, and a girl chum of the Smith girl were in the party.

They started from Redondo yesterday afternoon for Rocky Point, some miles away. On the return the engine went dead.

At daylight the launch was seen drifting helplessly off Hermosa beach. Rescuers found Ruth Smith unconscious from exposure and Mrs. Blake and Harriet Blake in a delirious condition.

The men worked all night bailing the boat to keep it afloat.

———o———

St. Louis Star & Times, December 17, 1914.

6 IN DISABLED LAUNCH ARE SWEPT OUT TO SEA

LOS ANGELES, CAL., Dec. 17.— Swept out to sea in a howling southeast gale, six persons, including two little girls, were believed to have perished last night off Redondo. The United States destroyer Preble, Lieut. Martin Metcalfe commanding, took up the search at daylight from San Pedro.

Those in the boat, all residents of Redondo, were:

Mr. and Mrs. J. H. Blake; Charles Blake, 22 years old; Harriet Blake, 17; Ruth Smith, 11.

Playmate of the latter girl, name unknown.

The Blake party left Redondo at 10 o'clock yesterday morning for Rocky Point in search of abalones. They had with them their 10-year-old son, Eugene, and were accompanied by Timothy Ozungia, a fisherman. Returning at 4:30 in the afternoon when five miles from Redondo the engine went dead.

Taking Eugene Blake in his skiff, Ozuniga rowed to Redondo for aid, while those on the launch threw out two twenty-five-pound anchors. The lunch Moon went out, but could find no trace of the disabled boat. After cruising over a radius of four miles, the Moon returned to Redondo and gave the news. A small fleet of launches immediately took to sea, but returned at midnight without having found a trace of the lost party.

The story below was printed in these local MO papers.: Harrison County Times, Kansas City Journal, New Hampton Herald, Plattsburg Leader, St. Joseph Gazette, The Concordian, The Corning Mirror, The Hardin News, The King City Chronicle, The Sarcoxie Record, and the Urich Herald Montrose Tidings.

These papers did not reprint the story: Smithville Democrat-Herald, owned by W.B. Harris, and Kansas City Star, owned by Harris' friend and colleague, Bill Nelson.

LOWER PACIFIC COAST STORM

Fisherman Lost From Launch That Went Out for Rescue—Over $100,000 Damage Done.

Los Angeles, Dec. 18.—Heavy seas, rolled up by a 40-mile wind along the southern coast, cost one life and wrought damage today amounting to more than $100,000 at Long Beach and at Hueneme.

John Caspinola, a fisherman, was lost off the launch Roma, which went out to search for a motor boat blown out to sea with six members of the family of J. H. Blake of Redondo. The Blakes, however, were saved by another vessel.

At Long Beach breakers dashed into the Strand, tearing out bulkheads and cement walks and wrecking several residences close to the water front.

At Hueneme a 1,000-foot section of a long wharf was smashed, causing damage estimated at $50,000.

Dr. Frank Hurwitt obit, Kansas City Times, Feb. 1, 1975. Hurwitt was a prominent physician in Kansas City who helped deliver Nona Mount-Blake's son.

Dr. Frank Hurwitt

Dr. Frank Hurwitt, 92, of 4401 Rockhill, died Friday at the Menorah Medical Center. He was born in New York.

Dr. Hurwitt was graduated in 1909 from Washington University in St. Louis. He was a member of the staffs at the Research Medical Center, the General Hospital and St. Luke's Hospital and was a member of the original staff of the Menorah Medical Center, where he was also chief of anesthesiology. He had an office in the Professional Building, 1103 Grand, before he retired about 25 years ago.

He commanded the only ambulance company from Kansas City to serve in the 1916 Mexican border skirmish. He was a captain. In World War I he was a physician

DR. FRANK HURWITT

with the U. S. Army Ambulance Company. He retired from active military service as a lieutenant colonel and moved here in 1919 when he was admitted to the Jackson County Medical Society.

During World War II Dr. Hurwitt was chairman of the national committee for the examination of federalized national guardsmen.

From 1912 to 1922 he was with the city health department and later was a physician for the welfare board here. In 1952 Dr. Hurwitt was appointed medical co-ordinator of the Missouri Civil Defense Agency. He was appointed in 1958 to the Zionist Organization of America delegation to the Israel Bond conference.

Dr. Hurwitt was certified by the American Board of Anesthesiology and was a member of the American Society of Anesthesiologists.

He was a member of the Scottish Rite Bodies and was a 32nd-degree mason. He was a charter member of Congregation B'nai Jehudah and was a member of B'nai B'rith.

He leaves a son, Irwin E. Hurwitt, and a daughter, Mrs. Fayette Unger, both of Kansas City; four grandchildren and eight great-grandchildren.

Services will be at 11:30 a.m. Sunday at the Louis Chapel; burial in Rose Hill Cemetery. The family suggests contributions to the Menorah Medical Center.

Pallbearers: David Frank Hurwitt, Donald Hurwitt Kasle, Philip Kinney and Myron E. Sildon.

Deaths Over Missouri

Lexington—Leslie Vernon Dryer, 56, Lexington, died Friday at the Lexington Memorial Hospital. He was born near Wellington, Mo., and had lived in Higginsville, Mo., and Lexington most of his life. Mr. Dryer was a farmer and a carpenter. He previously was a truck driver three years for the Lake City Army Ammunition Plant. He was an Army veteran of World War II and a life member of the Veterans of Foreign Wars. He was a member of the Lexington Masonic Lodge, the Lexington Chapter of the Royal Arch Masons and the DeMolay Commandry Knights Templar. He was a former member of the Lexington Turner Society and American Legion. He also was a member of the St. Luke's United Church of Christ, Wellington. He leaves his wife, Mrs. Virginia Dryer of the home; a son, Vernon Keith Dryer, rural Lexington; a daughter, Mrs. Mary Virginia Kopp, Lexington; two brothers, Will Lorry Dryer and Roger Dryer, both of Higginsville; two sisters, Mrs. Doris Triplett, Sibley in Jackson County, and Mrs. Winnie Knehans, rural Higginsville, and five grandchildren. Services will be at 2 p.m. Sunday at the church; burial in the church's cemetery. Friends may call after 7 p.m. tonight at the Vaughn-Walker Chapel here.

The Harrises

Portrait of Anna Mount, c. 1907, taken by Robert Alexander Wells (R. Alex Wells), a photographer in Higginsville, MO. Wells moved to Oklahoma City, OK in 1909, making way for A.T. Peterson.

W. B. Harris, formerly editor of the Kelly paper, was married at Higginsville, Mo, to Miss Anna Mount last week.

The Centralia Journal, Dec. 25, 1908

"Uncle Bernie" Harris of the Smithville Democrat-Herald achieved a new distinction when he carried away first honors in the recent spelling match there. "Uncle Bernie's" efforts in journalistic lines have been spelling success for him for some time and the other words are all easy after that.

Kansas City Times, April 24, 1916

Collins Kindred, postmaster at Smithville, has purchased the Democrat-Herald from W. B. Harris.

Kansas City Times, Dec. 26, 1918. In 1919, W.B. Harris, wife Anna, and son Howard moved back to Kansas City. They resided for a while on Monroe Ave., and then on Askew Ave. W.B. worked at several printing houses including Peerless Printing & Publishing, and Allen Stamp, Seal, & Manufacturing Co.

W.B Harris and Anna Mount-Harris, Kansas City, MO, c. 1940.

WARREN BERNARD HARRIS.

Rites to Be Held Saturday for Former Newspaperman.

Funeral services for Warren Bernard Harris, 74 years old, who died yesterday at his home, 1011 Prospect avenue, will be held at 4 o'clock Saturday at the Newcomer chapel.

Mr. Harris, from 1912 to 1920, was editor and owner of the Smithfield, Mo., Democrat-Herald, and worked on other

Warren B. Harris.

papers in Centralia and Seneca, Kas., and Higginsville, Mo.

In 1920 he came to Kansas City. From 1939 to 1949 he was with the Potts-Turnbull Advertising company. He also was associated with various printing firms here.

Mr. Harris leaves his wife, Mrs. Anna F. Harris of the home; a son, Howard B. Harris, Thirty-sixth street and Blue Ridge road; a daughter, Mrs. Bernice Fickenger, Washington, and four grandchildren.

W.B. Harris obit, Kansas City Star, April 20, 1951. Harris had a daughter from his first marriage to Gertrude Warner. When Gertrude died in 1905, their daughter Bernice remained in Kansas and was raised by her grandparents.

W.B. Harris' parents were Robert Harris & Lucy Rucker (married 1873). Robert Harris passed away in 1890, and Lucy Rucker remarried in 1893 to David Garver. The Garvers lived in Corning, Kansas. W.B. Harris visited his mother and his daughter occasionally. See below from <u>The Seneca Tribune</u> (Seneca, Kansas), May 31, 1917. Misprint of W.B. Harris as "B.W. Harris."

> B. W. Harris, wife and young son, of Smithville, Mo., were here last week, the guests of his mother, Mrs. Dave Garver. They came to attend the graduating exercises. His daughter Bernice was a member of the class of 1917 and has been making her home with her Grandma Garver. Harris is editor of a paper in Missouri. He was a member of the first class to graduate from the Corning high school, and a former editor of the Corning Gazette.

Portrait of Bernice Harris, daughter of W.B. Harris & Gertrude Warner, 1920s.

MRS. ANNA F. HARRIS

Mrs. Anna F. Harris, 87, of 23 Warner Plaza, died yesterday at the home. She was born in Higginsville, Mo., and had lived here 53 years. She leaves a son, Howard Harris, 9910 Delmar, Overland Park, and a sister, Mrs. Edna Sauvain, Salina, Kas.

Anna Mount-Harris Obit, <u>Kansas City Star</u>, Dec. 20, 1970

Warren B. Harris headstone, Forest Hill Cemetery, Kansas City, MO. Anna Mount-Harris was also buried at Forest Hill.

W. B. HARRIS. The best small town paper in Clay County is the distinction given by its readers and the general public to the Democrat-Herald at Smithville. Its editor and proprietor, W. B. Harris, is a newspaper man from the ground up, and has had little experience in any other field since boyhood.

W. B. Harris was born in Corning, Kansas, January 6, 1877, a son of Robert A. and Lucy (Rucker) Harris. His father, who was born in Indiana, moved out to Kansas in 1867, and homesteaded land in that state, where he lived the life of a practical farmer until his death in 1890 at the age of thirty-nine. He was the father of four children: W. B.; Roscoe, of Corning, Kansas; Inez, wife of Earl R. Short, of Colorado; and Robert, of Corning. The mother is now living at Corning as the wife of D. B. Garver.

While on the Kansas farm Mr. Harris attended school in town, and in 1893 finished the course in the high school at Corning. Two years before, in 1891, he began his newspaper apprenticeship in all-round work in the office of the Corning Gazette. On May 11, 1896, he attained to the dignity of proprietor by the purchase of a half interest in the plant, but a year later sold out and bought the Times at Vermillion, Kansas. After publishing it 3½ years, he moved the plant to Kelly, Kansas, and issued the Reporter, with which he was actively identified 3½ years. Following this Mr. Harris came to Missouri, and from March, 1905, to December, 1912, was foreman on the Jeffersonian at Higginsville. Since December, 1912, his home has been in Smithville, where he bought the Democrat-Herald.

Mr. Harris was reared a republican, but is now of the democratic party. He is affiliated with the Independent Order of Odd Fellows, the Knights of Pythias and the Mystic Workers of the World. His church is the Presbyterian, while Mrs. Harris is a Baptist. He was married March 8, 1898, to Miss Gertrude Warner, of Kansas. She died June 19, 1905, leaving a daughter, Bernice. December 12, 1908, Mr. Harris married Anna Mount, of Higginsville. Her parents are Charles and Samantha (Carel) Mount, the former a native of Alabama and the latter of Indiana, and both now residents of Kansas City, Missouri. Mr. and Mrs. Harris are the parents of one son, Howard.

A History of Northwest Missouri, Volume III by Walter Williams (Lewis Publishing Company. 1915); p. 2019-2020.

Howard Bernard Harris (son of W.B. & Anna), c. 1920

Howard B. Harris yearbook photo, Central Middle School, 1926;

Below: Howard B. Harris yearbook photo, Central High School 1929; Howard B. Harris riding a pinto horse and holding a clarinet as part of the KC Pinto Band, c. 1929.

HOWARD B. HARRIS

If there ever was a handsome "cowboy", here he is, for Howard is a member of the rough riding, hard playing "Pinto Band". Yes, he rides as well as he plays.

HOWARD B. HARRIS
1912-1981

The Kansas City Pinto Band,
led by "Tom Mix" in
photograph above.

Howard B. Harris married
Agnes C. Lynch in 1935.
<u>Kansas City Star</u>,
Nov. 29, 1935

A RECENT BRIDE.

—*Photograph by DeCloud's Studio.*
Mrs. Howard B. Harris, who, be-
fore her recent marriage, was
Miss Agnes Lynch, daughter of
Mr. and Mrs. H. J. Lynch.

Howard B. Harris & Agnes Lynch-Harris, 1930s.

WWII draft registration card for Howard B. Harris, listing his mother, Anna Floretta Harris, as his next of kin.

HARRIS—Howard B. Harris II, 6 months old, died yesterday at the St. Joseph hospital. He had been ill about a week. He leaves his parents, Mr. and Mrs. Howard B. Harris, 2913 East Twenty-eighth street. Funeral services will be held at 9:30 o'clock Tuesday at the Newcomer chapel and at 10 o'clock at the Annunciation Catholic church; burial in Calvary cemetery.

Howard B. Harris & Agnes Lynch-Harris' first child passed away at 6 months old on March 6, 1938. Kansas City Times, March 6, 1938. They would have two girls, Sandra (born 1940) and Marci (born 1945).

The Sauvains

Guy P. Sauvain and Edna Mount-Sauvain visiting San Fernando, CA, 1920s.

SAUVAIN—John William Sauvain, 821 East Thirty-eighth street, died yesterday in Grace hospital. He was 67 years old and was a Mason. The survivors: Three sons, P. G. Sauvain, St Joseph, Mo.; G. P. Sauvain and J. C. Sauvain, both of 2315 Montgall avenue, and two daughters, Mrs. F. H. Dincoe, Higginsville, Mo., and Mrs. Hal Skeely, New York City. Funeral services will be at 2 o'clock tomorrow afternoon in Mrs. C. L. Forster's chapel.

Obit for John W. Sauvain, listing his children with Laura (Prosser) Sauvain-Schooling: Paul G. Sauvain, Guy P. Sauvain, J. Clyde Sauvain, and Eunice Sauvain-Skelly (Mrs. Hal Skelly). A "Mrs. F.H. Dincoe" is also listed, who may be a daughter from a later marriage.

The Garden City store will be conducted along the same lines that has been so successful in Liberal. In the center room of the Haskell building will be installed a modern electric shoe repair shop. This business will be owned by G. P. Sauvain, who comes here from Kansas City. Mr. and Mrs. Sauvain arrived this week and Mr. Sauvain is now arranging for the installation of his equipment. The rear of the room occupied by Mr. Sauvain will be used for a sample room.

Guy P. Sauvain and wife Edna Mount-Sauvain moved to Garden City, Kansas in 1929. Garden City News, Sept. 5, 1929.

> Guy Sauvain accompanied his mother, Mrs. L. Schooling to Kansas City Sunday and is spending the week visiting and transacting business there. Mrs. Schooling has been a guest in the Sauvain home for a few weeks. During Mr. Sauvain's absence C. W. Buchfink has charge of the Goodyear Shoe Shop.

Above: Guy P. Sauvain worked in shoes sales & repair for his entire career. In 1930, he managed the Goodyear Shoe Shop. This article states that he spent time in Kansas City, MO with his mother, Laura Schooling. Garden City News, June 19, 1930.

Below: The Sauvains traveled between Garden City & Salina, Kansas and Kansas City, MO frequently to visit family. In the 1930s, Guy and Edna traveled to visit Charles S. Mount (Edna's father) and Frank Hurwitt Blake (Edna's nephew). Charles Mount and Frank Hurwitt Blake visited with the Sauvains in Kansas as well. Thayer Howard was a fellow shoe salesman. Garden City News, Aug. 21, 1930.

> Guy Sauvain and Thayer Howard returned Wednesday from Kansas City where they have been several days. They were accompanied home by Mrs. Sauvain's father, Charles Mount and her nephew, Hurwitt Blake, who will remain here several weeks.

On their wedding day, Mr. and Mrs. G. P. Sauvain.

Mr. and Mrs. G. P. Sauvain

Sauvains married 55 years

Mr. and Mrs. G. P. Sauvain, 673 S. 12th, entertained with a dinner party in observance of their 55th wedding anniversary at the downtown Elks club.

The couple was wed April 17, 1917 in Kansas City, Mo., and has lived in Salina 37 years. Sauvain is a shoe repairman at the George Seitz Shoe company.

Attending the dinner were Mssrs. and Mmes. Roger Fink, Fred Wilson, Joe Crawford, William Duncan, Wallace Urmey, Stanley Shivers, Jack Barrett and Mrs. Helen Witt and Sam Chaltas, all of Salina.

Guy P. Sauvain &
Edna Mount-Sauvain
had a long and happy
marriage. In 1972,
they celebrated their
55th wedding
anniversary.
Salina Journal,
April 21, 1972.

In 1974, in his eighties, Guy P. Sauvain continued to work in shoe repair. He decided he did not like retirement, so he became manager of Seitz Shoe Co. in Salina, Kansas. Top: Salina Journal, Feb. 25, 1974; bottom: Salina Journal, Oct. 2, 1978.

Alex Benoit, a deaf-mute, was the Seitz repairman for 49 years until his death in the early 1960s. Today repairs are done by 86-year-old Guy Sauvain, who got bored after 10 years of retirement and returned to the cobbler's bench.

need someone to look up to.

Mr. and Mrs. Guy Sauvain

62nd date
for Sauvains

Tuesday will be the 62nd wedding anniversary of Mr. and Mrs. Guy Sauvain,
673 S. 12th. No formal celebration is
planned.

The celebrants were united in mar-
riage April 17, 1917, in Kansas City, Mo.
Mrs. Sauvain is the former Edna
Mount.

They have lived in Salina for the past
40 years. Sauvain has been a shoe repairman for 70 years. He works for
Seitz Shoe Co.

Guy P. Sauvain &
Edna Mount-Sauvain
celebrated their 62nd
wedding anniversary
in 1979.
Salina Journal,
April 16, 1979.

MRS. GUY P. SAUVAIN
The funeral for Mrs. Edna Sauvain, 90, 673 S. 12th, will be at 1 p.m. Saturday at the Ryan Mortuary, the Rev. Herman Van Arsdale officiating.

Mrs. Sauvain died Wednesday at Asbury Hospital. She was born Nov. 7, 1887, at Higginsville, Mo., and came to Salina in 1974. For many years, she and her husband, Guy P., who survives, operated the Star Shoe Shop. She was a member of the Salina Elks Auxiliary.

Besides her husband, survivors are nephews and nieces.

Burial will be in Gypsum Hill Cemetery.

Obit for Edna Mount-Sauvain, <u>Salina Journal</u>, Feb. 8, 1980.

Edna Mount- Sauvain, & Guy P. Sauvain (GYPSUM HILL CEMETERY) SALINA, KANSAS

Death certificate for G.P. Sauvain, the husband of Edna Mount, on May 14, 1985, at age 92 of cardiopulmonary arrest while at Windsor Estates Nursing Home in Salina, Kansas. Mrs. Agnes Harris (Howard B. Harris' wife) was the informant on the death certificate.

The Newmans

Stella Mount, the third child of Charles and Samantha Mount, married Fred Newman in 1895. They had four children: Orville (b. 1896, d. 1954), Eva (b. 1899, d. 1963), Dorothy (b. 1905, d. 1995), and Freddie (b. 1907, d. 1997). The Newmans were a prominent Higginsville, Missouri family. Orville and Eva had their portraits taken by A.T. Peterson in 1910.

Orville Newman

Eva Newman

The Sebastians

Belle Mount, the second child of Charles and Samantha Mount, married Richard M. Sebastian in 1891. They had seven children: Charles (b. 1891, d. 1942), Edith (b. 1894, d. 1988), William (b. 1895, d. 1972), Elizabeth (b. 1899, d. 1981), Thelma (b. 1904, d. 1980), Richard A. (b. 1907, d. 1971), and Edwin (b. 1911, d. 1944). The Sebastians were another prominent Higginsville, Missouri family.

Richard M. Sebastian & Belle Mount-Sebastian, c. 1910

Charles S. Sebastian—Word has been reecived here of the death last night of Mr. Sebastian, former resident of Kansas City, at Ramcna, Cal., where he had lived the last four months. He was injured Sunday night in an automobile accident near Ramona.

Mr. Sebastian, a foreman for the Union Pacific Railroad, lived here 20 years. Survivors are his wife, Mrs. Mina Sebastian, of the home; two sons, James R., Lake Tapawingo, and Gene, Crystal City, Mo.; his mother, Mrs. Belle Sebastian, Corder, Mo.; three brothers, Edwin, 2107 E. 79th St.; Richard, North Platte, Neb., and William G., Windsor, Mo., and three sisters, Mrs. Edith Livesay, 4015 Forest Ave.; Mrs. Albert Schole, Concordia, Mo., and Mrs. Thelma Branch, Corder.

Charles S. Sebastian portrait, c. 1913

Obit, Kansas City Journal, Jan. 20, 1942. Sons James and Gene are from his first marriage to Gertrude A. Kincheloe.

James R. Sebastian (son of Charles S. Sebastian) as child in 1913; as adult in 1930.

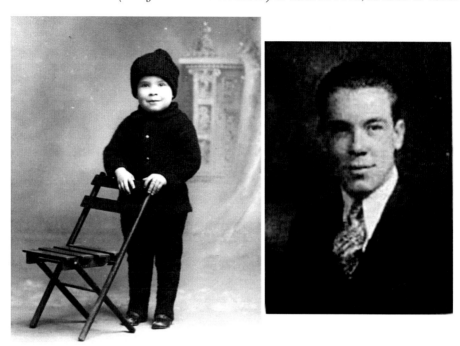

The *"Eastonian,"* the yearbook for East High School in Kansas City, featuring first team football. J.R. Sebastian was on the football and basketball team.

Edith Sebastian-Livesay, c. 1942

*William Sebastian
(man on the right),
WWI military,
c. 1919*

Elizabeth Sebastian - Scholle, c. 1942

Thelma Sebastian, c. 1920

Richard A. Sebastian as toddler in 1911; as adult in 1942

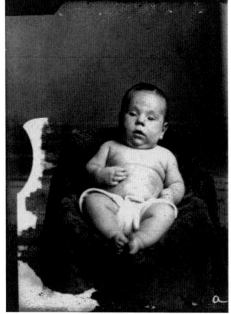

Edwin B. Sebastian as infant in 1911; as adult in c. 1920s

Sebastian family photo, c. 1942

BIBLIOGRAPHY

A NOTE ON SOURCES

The sources referenced in the footnotes throughout this book are largely the primary and secondary sources listed below. Many of the documents and photographs, however, are from the author's collection of Mount-Harris-Sebastian-Blake family archives.

PRIMARY SOURCES

Manuscript Collections

Cornell University Division of Rare & Manuscript Collections
"Dawn's Early Light: The First 50 Years of American Photography; Exhibition: Photographic Processes: 1839 – 1889 DRY PLATE NEGATIVE (gelatin dry plate), 1880-1920, https://rmc.library.cornell.edu/DawnsEarlyLight/exhibition/process es/dry_plate_neg.html.

University of California, San Diego Special Collections & Archives: Lee Shippey Papers

Photograph/Art Collections

Kansas City Public Library Digital Collections

Kansas City Public Library Digital History: The Pendergast Years

Oregon State University: Early Photographic Formats and Processes in the Special Collections and Archives Research Center

State Historical Society of Missouri: Ruth B. Bush Postcard Collection

State Historical Society of Missouri-Columbia: Leonard D. and Marie H. Rehkop Collection of Algert T. Peterson Photographs

University of Iowa digital collection, "Traveling Culture: Circuit Chautauqua in the Twentieth Century." digital.lib.uiowa.edu/tc/

Archives & Databases

Ancestry.com
  California, U.S., County Birth, Marriage, and Death Records, 1849-1980

  Kansas, U.S., County Marriage Records, 1811-1911

  U.S., City Directories, 1822-1995

  U.S., School Yearbooks, 1880-2012

California Department of Health Services
  California Birth Index, 1905-1995 (Sacramento, CA)

Kansas State Archives
  Kansas Adjutant General. *Armed Forces Personnel Who Served Between September 16, 1940, and June 30, 1946.*

Library of Congress
  Chronicling America: Historic American Newspapers

  Grand Army of the Republic and Kindred Societies: A Guide to Resources in the General Collections of the Library of Congress

  Prints and Photographs Division: Panoramic Photographs; National Photo Company Collection

Missouri Office of the Secretary of State
  Missouri Death Certificates, 1910-1969

Missouri State Archives
  Missouri Marriage Records. Jefferson City, MO

National Archives at St. Louis, MO
  WWII Draft Registration Cards For Missouri, 10/16/1940-03/31/1947; Record Group: Records of the Selective Service System, 147; Box: 135

National Archives & Records Administration
> Records of the Bureau of Marine Inspection and Navigation.
> *Merchant Marine Applications for Licenses of Officers.* Records of the U.S.
> Coast Guard, Record Group 26.

> Records of the Department of Veterans Affairs. *Special Schedules of the Eleventh Census (1890) Enumerating Union Veterans and Widows of Union Veterans of the Civil War*, Series Number: M123; Record Group Title; Record Group Number: 15; Census Year: 1890

> United States of America, Bureau of the Census: *Census records 1880-1980*

> United States, Selective Service System. *World War I Selective Service System Draft Registration Cards, 1917-1918.*

U.S., Newspapers.com

Roy Rosenzweig Center for History and New Media (CHNM) at George Mason University and the University of Missouri–Kansas City: *Children and Youth in History.*

Newspapers

The Buffalo Courier (Buffalo, NY)

The Catholic Tribune (St. Joseph, MO)

Chilhowee News (Chilhowee, MO)

Columbia Missourian (Columbia, MO)

The Concordian (Concordia, MO)

The Corning Gazette (Corning, Kansas)

The Garden City News (Garden City, Kansas)

The Henry County Republican (Clinton, MO)

Higginsville Advance (Higginsville, MO)

Higginsville Jeffersonian (Higginsville, MO)

Johnson County Star (Johnson County, MO)

Kansas City Journal (Kansas City, MO)

The Kansas City Post (Kansas City, MO)

Kansas City Star (Kansas City, MO)

Kansas City Times (Kansas City, MO)

King City Democrat (King City, MO)

The La Belle Star (La Belle, MO)

The Lathrop Optimist (Lathrop, MO)

Lebanon-Rustic Republican (Lebanon, MO)

The Lexington Intelligencer (Lexington, MO)

Los Angeles Evening Express (Los Angeles, CA)

Los Angeles Times (Los Angeles, CA)

The Marshall Republican (Marshall, MO)

The Maryville Daily Forum (Maryville, MO)

Redondo Reflex (Redondo Beach, CA)

The Reporter (The Kelly Reporter) (Kelly, Kansas)

The Salina Journal (Salina, Kansas)

Saline County Weekly Progress (Marshall, MO)

San Pedro Daily Pilot (San Pedro, CA)

San Pedro News Pilot (San Pedro, CA)

San Pedro Today (San Pedro, CA)

Smithville Democrat-Herald (Smithville, MO)

St. Joseph-Gazette (St. Joseph, MO)

St. Joseph News Press Gazette (St. Joseph, MO)

Warrenton Volksfreund (Warrenton, MO)

Weekly Democrat Forum (Maryville, MO)

Printed Works

Jackson County Historical Society, *An Illustrated Description of Independence, MO* (Jackson County, MO: 1902)

Otis Elevator Company, *Otis Elevator Company: the Otis elevator industry comprises large manufacturing plants in the principal cities in the United States, Canada, Great Britain, Germany and France* (1903)

Otis Elevator Company, *Moving your customers and what they buy. brief suggestions for increasing business by improving service* (1915)

Otis Elevator Company, *Otis hand power elevators* (1920)

Otis Elevator Company, *The first one hundred years* (1953)

Staff of the Kansas City Star, *William Rockhill Nelson: The Story of a Man, a Newspaper and a City* (Kansas City, Missouri: 1915)

Local, State, & Federal Documents

Bielefeldt, Vi and Janice McMillian, *Historic and Architectural Survey of Higginsville, Missouri* (Show-Me Regional Planning Commission & Missouri Office of Historic Preservation: 1982)

California State Fisheries Laboratory, et. al., *The Scientific Investigation of Marine Fisheries: As Related to the Work of the Fish and Game Commission in Southern California, Volumes 1-11* (California State Printing Office, Jan. 1913)

U.S. Census Bureau, *Sixteenth Census of the United States, 1940: Comparative Occupation Statistics for the U.S., 1870-1940* (Washington, D.C., Government Printing Office: 1943)

United States Department of the Interior: National Park Service, *National Register of Historic Places: Graphic Arts Building, Jackson County, Missouri* (Architectural and Historical Research, LLC, Kansas City, MO: 2005)

United States Department of the Interior, National Park Service, *National Register of Historic Places Registration form for Central Embarcadero Piers Historic District, Piers 1, 1 ½ , 3, 5* (California Office of Historic Preservation, San Francisco, CA: 2002)

"Standards and Certification Chronology: Defining Events in ASME Standards & Certification" ASME Standards and Certification Chronology, accessed May 9, 2024, https://www.asme.org/codes-standards/about-standards/history-of-asme-standards/codes-and-standards-chronology

SECONDARY SOURCES

Books

__*The Encyclopedia Americana* (New York, Chicago: The Encyclopedia American corporation: 1904 and 1918 editions).

Draper, Mary Joe, *Kansas City's Historic Midtown Neighborhoods* (Arcadia Publishing, 2015)

Estabrooke, Edward M., *Photography in the Studio and in the Field* (E. & H.T. Anthony & Company: 1887)

Hoe, Robert, *A short history of the printing press: and of the improvements in printing machinery from the time of Gutenberg up to the present day* (New York, 1902)

Larsen, Lawrence H. and Nancy J. Hulston, *Pendergast!* (University of Missouri Press, 2016)

Love, Milton S., *The Ecology of Marine Fishes: California and Adjacent Waters* (University of California Press, Berkeley, 2006)

Misiroglu, Gina, *American Countercultures: An Encyclopedia of Nonconformists, Alternative Lifestyles, and Radical Ideas in U.S. History* (Routledge, 2015)

Odem, Mary E., *Delinquent Daughters: Protecting and Policing Adolescent Female Sexuality in the United States, 1885-1920* (University of North Carolina Press: 2000)

Shortridge, James R., *Kansas City and How It Grew, 1822–2011* (University Press of Kansas, 2012)

Spletsoser, Frederick and Lawrence Larsen, *Kansas City: 100 Years of Business* (Kansas City, Kansas City Journal: 1988)

Williams, Walter, ed., *A History of Northwest Missouri: Volume 2*, (The Lewis Publishing Company, 1915)

Young, William, *Youngs history of Lafayette County, Missouri* (Indianapolis, IN: B.F. Bowen & Co., 1910)

Articles & Theses

Caporale, Robert S., "North American Elevator Industry Codes and Standards: A history on the governing standard in North America and explanation of how it is put together," *Elevator World* (March 2016)

Claro, Lyndsey, "Women in the gentleman's career of publishing." Princeton University Press. March 6, 2020. https://press.princeton.edu/ideas/women-in-the-gentlemans-career-of-publishing

Hansan, John E., "The Pendergast Machine of Kansas City, Missouri (1900-1939)," *Social Welfare History Project*. 2011. https://socialwelfare.library.vcu.edu/people/pendergast-machine/

Harper, Kimberly, Stephanie Kukuljan, and John W. McKerley, "Historic Missourians: Thomas J. Pendergast." State Historical Society of Missouri. https://historicmissourians.shsmo.org/thomas-pendergast

Lieber, Ruth Evaline, "The Kansas City star as a social force," (Bachelor of Arts Thesis, University of Illinois, 1918).

U.S. Department of the Interior, National Park Service, "Central Embarcadero Piers Historic District", https://www.nps.gov/places/central-embarcadero-piers-historic-district.htm

Video/Alternative Media

Jack Baric, "The Smell of Money: The Story of the Fishing and Canning Industry of the Los Angeles Harbor Area," (Port of Los Angeles: 2024). Documentary. Port of Los Angeles Youtube: https://www.youtube.com/watch?v=D_Fzv6T6YWk&t=70s

CHARACTER LIST

BLAKE, ADA E.: Wife of James H. Blake

BLAKE, CHARLES A.: Son of James H. Blake & Ada E. Blake; husband to Nona Mount-Blake (1st wife) & Evelyn Miller-Blake (2nd wife)

BLAKE, FRANK HURWITT: Son of Charles A. Blake & Nona Mount-Blake

BLAKE, JAMES H.: Husband of Ada E. Blake

BLAKE, THEODORE: Son of James H. Blake & Ada E. Blake

BLAKE-CARTER, SHARON: Daughter of Frank H. Blake & Lorraine Alsace Derby

BLAKE-CROY, HARRIET: Daughter of James H. Blake & Ada E. Blake; wife of Harold Croy

BLAKE-MILLER, MICHELE: Daughter of Frank H. Blake & Lorraine Alsace Derby

CAMPBELL, WILLIAM N.: Co-proprietor of Campbell-Gates Printing Co.

COE, JULIUS G.: Early editor of the *Higginsville Jeffersonian*

CROY, HAROLD: Husband of Harriet Blake-Croy

CROY, VIVIAN MAY: Daughter of Harold Croy & Harriet Blake-Croy

DERBY, LORRAINE ALSACE: Wife of Frank H. Blake

FULTON, BOYD A.: Office boy for John Reed Printing Co.

GATES, GEORGE W.: Co-proprietor of Campbell-Gates Printing Co.

GROVE, BENJAMIN F.: Janitor & extra elevator operator for Graphic Arts Building

HARRIS, HOWARD B.: Son of Warren B. Harris & Anna Mount-Harris

HARRIS, WARREN B.: Husband of Anna Mount-Harris; proprietor of the *Smithville Democrat-Herald*

HURWITT, FRANK (DR.): Physician in Kansas City, MO; assisted in delivering baby Frank H. Blake to Nona Mount-Blake

KELLY, JAMES A.: 2nd husband of Evelyn Miller-Blake

LIVESAY, EDWIN FORREST: Husband of Edith Sebastian-Livesay; co-proprietor of the *Smithville Democrat-Herald*

LIVESAY, LETA BELLE: Daughter of E.F. Livesay & Edith Sebastian-Livesay

LIVESAY, ROBERT: Son of E.F. Livesay & Edith Sebastian-Livesay

LIVESAY, WILLIAM: Father of E.F. Livesay

MILLER, WILLIAM H.: 1st husband of Kathryn (Wilson) Miller-Whitney; father of Evelyn Miller-Blake

MILLER-BLAKE, EVELYN: Daughter of William H. Miller & Kathryn (Wilson) Miller-Whitney; 2nd wife of Charles A. Blake

MOUNT, CHARLES S.: Husband of Samantha Mount; patriarch of Mount family

MOUNT, ELIZABETH: Fourth child of Charles S. Mount & Samantha Mount

MOUNT, MAMIE: Sixth child of Charles S. Mount & Samantha Mount

MOUNT, SAMANTHA: Wife of Charles S. Mount; matriarch of the Mount family

MOUNT, STELLA: Third child of Charles S. Mount & Samantha Mount

MOUNT, WILLIAM T.: First child of Charles S. Mount & Samantha Mount

MOUNT-BLAKE, NONA L.: Eighth child of Charles S. Mount & Samantha Mount; 1st wife of Charles A. Blake; mother of Frank H. Blake

MOUNT-HARRIS, ANNA; Fifth child of Charles S. Mount & Samantha Mount; wife of Warren B. Harris; mother of Howard B. Harris

MOUNT-SAUVAIN, EDNA: Seventh child of Charles S. Mount & Samantha Mount; wife of Frank J. Stamm (1st) and Guy P. Sauvain (2nd)

MOUNT-SEBASTIAN, BELLE: Second child of Charles S. Mount & Samantha Mount; wife of Richard M. Sebastian

NELSON, WILLIAM R.: Proprietor of the *Kansas City Star* & *Kansas City Times*; Republican

PENDERGAST, JAMES F.: Brother of Thomas J. Pendergast; first Democratic "political boss" in Kansas City, MO

PENDERGAST, THOMAS J.: Democratic "political boss" of Kansas City, MO, 1911-1939

PETERSON, ALGERT T.: Higginsville, MO photographer, 1909-1959

PETERSON, ANGNETTE: Wife of Algert T. Peterson

PETERSON, ANNA LOUISE: Daughter of Algert T. Peterson & Angnette Peterson

(PROSSER) SAUVAIN-SCHOOLING, LAURA: Wife of John W. Sauvain (1st) and Charles Schooling (2nd)

SEBASTIAN, RICHARD M.: Husband of Belle Mount-Sebastian

SEBASTIAN-LIVESAY, EDITH: Daughter of Richard A. Sebastian & Belle Mount-Sebastian; wife of Edwin Forrest Livesay

SHIPPEY, LEE: Editor of the *Higginsville Jeffersonian*, contributor to *Kansas City Star*, and contributor to *Los Angeles Times*; public speaker and poet

SAUVAIN, CLYDE: Son of John W. Sauvain & Laura (Prosser) Sauvain-Schooling

SAUVAIN, EUNICE: Daughter of John W. Sauvain & Laura (Prosser) Sauvain-Schooling

SAUVAIN, GUY P.: Son of John W. Sauvain & Laura (Prosser) Sauvain-Schooling; husband of Edna Mount-Sauvain

SAUVAIN, JOHN W.: 1st husband of Laura (Prosser) Sauvain-Schooling

SAUVAIN, PHILIP G.: Son of John W. Sauvain & Laura (Prosser) Sauvain-Schooling

SCHOOLING, CHARLES: 2nd husband of Laura (Prosser) Sauvain-Schooling

STAMM, FRANK J.: 1st husband of Edna Mount-Sauvain

TARBET, SAMUEL: Architect in Kansas City, MO; architect of Graphic Arts Building

THOMPSON, CORRELIA M.: Wife of Edwin H.L. Thompson

THOMPSON, EDWIN H.L.: Co-proprietor of Pratt-Thompson Investment & Construction Co.; husband of Correlia M. Thompson

WALLACE, GEORGE L.: Manager of Graphic Arts Building

(WILSON) MILLER-WHITNEY, KATHRYN: Wife of William H. Miller (1st) & Willard W. Whitney (2nd); mother of Evelyn Miller-Blake

ABOUT THE AUTHOR

Sarah J. Gross is an attorney and educator with publications in various journals including the *USC Interdisciplinary Law Journal* and the *Missouri Historical Review*. While living on campus at the University of California, Davis, Sarah graduated with a Bachelor's Degree in English and a minor in Expository Writing. She stayed on at Davis to receive a teaching credential and Master's Degree in Education, and then taught advanced English studies to middle school and high school students.

Sarah graduated from Chapman University Fowler School of Law in 2017 and passed the CA State Bar the same year. Following her bar admission, she lived on campus at Pepperdine University Caruso School of Law and graduated with an advanced law degree, a Master of Law (LL.M.). Sarah enjoys researching her family tree, and has ancestors who have lived in the state of Missouri since the late 1700's.

Made in the USA
Columbia, SC
24 June 2024